T0148399

Black Man With a Gun

Justifiable Force is a Constitutional Right

Lucky Rosenbloom

iUniverse, Inc.
Bloomington

Black Man With a Gun
Justifiable Force is a Constitutional Right

iUniverse books may be ordered through booksellers or by contacting:

iUniverse
1663 Liberty Drive
Bloomington, IN 47403
www.iuniverse.com
1-800-Authors (1-800-288-4677)

ISBN: 978-1-4502-9212-2 (pbk)
ISBN: 978-1-4502-9213-9 (ebk)

Printed in the United States of America

iUniverse rev. date: 4/20/2011

Contents

Preface

Black Folks can't blame Bush anymore

Here I am, sitting in my music room surrounded by drum machines, electronic keyboards, high-powered amps, music sheets and stuff like this — you know musician stuff. I must write a tune with a good hook to celebrate Obama's presidency. Should the movement be in 2/4, 3/4, 5/4, or 4/4?

The tempo is also integral to capturing attention. Can't be too fast and/or too slow? I'll need a hook that people can catch onto. Let me go with the regular 4/4 for soul. My hook: "Can't blame Bush anymore."

I am ready for the lyrics. Don't forget the hook, "Can't blame Bush anymore." Do you remember attending meetings within local Black organizations and hearing leaders blame Bush for their not being able to do anything to move the Black community forward? Hit it — "Can't blame Bush anymore."

I remember listening to a group of students, some high on drugs, reporting to school late, blaming Bush for not having enough credits to graduate and acting as though they had no reason to try because life seemed useless under the Bush administration. Hit it — "Can't blame Bush anymore."

Come on now. Think a moment for yourselves. Think of all the people, all the meetings you've attended over the years and heard people blame Bush for their setbacks. Hit it — "Can't blame Bush anymore."

So, tell me, as Black leaders and members of Black organizations, who are you going to blame? Hit it — "Can't blame Bush anymore."

You heard it here first. Liberals by the end of summer 2009 will place blame on Obama as they did Bush. The blame Obama game has already started. The blame Obama may not work. You see, Obama promotes self-reliance. Obama is the antithesis of everything molded around group failure, group victims, preferences, entitlements, and dependency programs that some Black leaders continue to advocate to promote and gain from victimhood. Obama is a Republican. You heard it here first.

As Obama moves closer to the center, as Obama makes good on his comment to end social programs that do not work, Obama will become the new justification of blame for those liberals having membership in agencies failing our communities.

I said it here first. The new blame will shift to Obama because — hit it — "Can't blame Bush anymore."

I believe that Obama is going to be in battle with the Affirmative Action liberal Blacks, such as Jesse Jackson. Remember the microphone incident?

Let me continue. Obama is going to be in battle with people like Jackson and Sharpton because Obama understands that repentance liberalism is the second White Southern Democrat betrayal of Black people leading to oppression and Black delusion. From this reality, Blacks, hit it — "Can't Blame Bush anymore" — will remain quiet, or shift blame towards Obama for their inability to reorganize the Black dependency on government back into focus.

I believe that Obama will continue to move Blacks beyond welfare and handouts because he knows that both welfare and Affirmative Action robs people of full responsibility and self-reliance. Obama knows that some social programs omit Black respect because some social programs promote inner inferiority. The reality is that many of these types of social programs destroying Black pride started with Clinton. It will be worth watching to see the shift of blame as liberal Blacks become more aware of the Obama dichotomy. Hit it — "Can't blame Bush anymore."

Let's talk about taxes. We never could blame Bush for this one because Republicans are about holding down taxes. However, let us look at the Obama's tax plan. Obama's tax plan means nothing as local Democrats raise property and other taxes to support big spending. Almost forgot my hook. Hit it — "Can't blame Bush anymore."

Under Obama, if you earn less than 19k, you should save $567. At 19-37k, there is about $892 in savings. Here is the problem at 66k-111k. With the savings, you'll never see the money. My bad. You will see the savings long enough to pay out the local raised taxes by your favorite Democrats.

When this happens, hit it — "Can't Blame Bush anymore." I'll stop my song for now. However, not to worry, more lyrics shall come soon.

Council on Black Minnesotans

Attending a meeting at the CBM, a group of Black youth presented their idea for wanting to have a primary-seatbelt law in Minnesota. The youth's research showed that such a law would lower the number of Blacks being killed in car accidents in urban America.

After the youth left the meeting, some CBMers indicated the law would be used for racial profiling, allowing police to pull Black youth over discovering drugs in their cars. This is the most stupid argument yet.

The police have more reasons to pull a person over without the primary-seatbelt law. Furthermore, Black youth should not be driving while smoking weed, drinking, or with weapons in their cars anyway. Not to mention the youth fighting for the bill are all Black.

Minnesota Democrats work to block Black vote by killing Identification bill

Blacks and women have fought hard to augment our right to vote. The Democrats diminished that right by voting down a Bill that would have empowered Black and Women voting rights.

I have seen Blacks walk away and not return to vote because of not having a utility bill needed to vote in Minnesota. The law enforcing ones right to vote by having proper identification would have taken away this abuse and empowered Blacks and women in urban Minnesota because this proper identification would have empowered the voter by not being turned away. How many of you carry a utility bill daily opposed to your identification?

Testifying in front of Democrats for this bill, allowed me to feel what it must have been like for Blacks to testify and fight Democrats like Gov. George Wallace and Bull Conner that were against the Civil Rights movement and voting rights for Blacks. Wallace and Conner would have been proud of the performance of each Democrat that voted the voter I.D. bill down in Minnesota. See my testimony regarding this matter at Youtube.com. Just type Lucky Rosenbloom in the search window.

Black Man With a Gun

Opinion 1

White liberals didn't mess with Muslims

We have learned in history lessons about the assassination of many civil rights leaders and workers at the hands of vicious, cruel and evil people during the Civil Rights Movement. However, when it came to Malcolm X, it was not the Whites but Blacks who killed this man of self-reliance.

You see, if a White had killed Malcolm, well, we would have seen retaliation in the streets unlike that for any other Black leader. This is the reason White liberals did not bother Malcolm and/or harass, rape or disrespect Muslim women during the struggle for civil rights.

In many of Malcolm's speeches he used the words "White liberals." In all the speeches I've listened to, I cannot find one wherein Malcolm uses any phrase such as "White conservatives." Listen to Malcolm's speeches and you will hear repeated references to White liberals. In fact, Malcolm has one speech titled "White Liberals."

Listen to Brother Malcolm's teachings and you shall gain wisdom about White liberals. Then, if you look closely in our community today, you would not be surprised to find that high-ranking officers in the Minneapolis Police Department have filed a discrimination lawsuit in liberal Minneapolis.

Black leaders have battled White liberals in our community for years. It's the White liberals who have historically entered the Black woman's home, taken her children, and placed them in homes with Whites who had no idea how to raise Black children. White liberals introduced welfare into the Black family and would later call Blacks shiftless and lazy; wanting to do nothing other than have babies and collects welfare.

It was White Democrats who created the Ku Klux Klan and fought to keep Blacks in slavery. When Malcolm talked about lynchings, murder, Black Codes and Jim Crow laws from 1870-1930, which were used to deny our rights as citizens, he was fully aware that Democrats were behind such evils. Presidents Roosevelt and Truman rejected anti-lynching laws and efforts to establish a permanent Civil Rights Commission.

Malcolm X spoke the truth about White liberals, but we continue to have leaders and so-called Black historians in our community today who act like house dancers, not house Negros, and who continue to tell you that

Republicans are our enemies. Republicans are not in our community; White liberals are.

I read an article wherein Black leaders accused Mayor R.T. Rybak of retaliation, responsible for the Minneapolis Urban League not getting a large amount of money to help Black youth. The mayor is a liberal.

I have witnessed, and so have you, battles for years in our community with White liberals towards justice and equality. There is a reason why White liberals don't play these kinds of games with Muslims — Black Muslims have not been blinded by White liberals and do not survive on their social dependency programs. In fact, I have never heard a Black Muslim beg a White liberal for anything or preach doom when a Republican is in office.

We're talking about White liberals such as Sen. Robert Byrd, who was a member of the KKK; or Sen. Hollings, who hoisted the Confederate flag over the South Carolina State Capitol; and Ted Kennedy, who called Black judicial nominees "Neanderthals." If Malcolm were with us today, he would talk about Al Gore's father and other White Liberals voting against the Civil Rights Act of the 1964.

And not one White Liberal would touch Malcolm.

Ramsey County sheriff and racial profiling

It's my intent to keep you informed regarding an incident of racial profiling in Little Canada in which this columnist was stopped by a Ramsey County deputy while riding my motorcycle during this deputy's so-called investigation of a person ripping off benches.

I have filed a complaint with the State Department of Human Rights. This department has been known to dismiss complaints with No Probable Cause findings. Two of these dismissals would later lead into court hearings wherein a judge issued findings in favor of the victim and another case settled.

So, let us see what this department does with a racial profiling incident as clear as the complaint this columnist has filed. If you have not followed my previous columns, call for a copy of the complaint and more details about the incident.

Lucky Rosenbloom welcomes reader responses to 612-661-0923, or email him at l.rosenbloom@yahoo.com

Opinion 2

I'm switching to the Democratic Party

In our last column ["Racial profiling; or, stupid behavior," *MSR* November 8], we provided a letter to Ramsey County Sheriff Bob Fletcher regarding this columnist being the subject of racial profiling in a predominantly White Little Canada while looking at real property. You, our readers, were given the content of that letter sent to Mr. Fletcher.

It is our desire to have you track the process from start to completion regarding this matter. As such, the following is the content of a letter received from Mr. Fletcher's office dated November 2, 2007:

"The Ramsey County Sheriff's Department, Internal Affairs Office has received your faxed complaint regarding the incident that occurred on the morning of October 20, 2007 in the city of Little Canada. We appreciate you bringing your complaint forward so that this matter can be thoroughly investigated. At this point, we expect to have a response to you by the end of the month. Thank you again for bringing this matter to our attention."

The above response is the definition of the word "placate." Signed by Commander Brenda Brozik of the Internal Affairs Office, the commander should have taken the risk and concluded something like, "By the way, Lucky, we would like for you to be a part of our training. You see, we are going to start our motorcycle patrol. With the skills you have at stealing benches using your motorcycle as transportation, man, we could use those kinds of skills around here."

We will keep you the reader advised of this so-called investigation in our upcoming columns.

I'm changing to a Democrat

After careful consideration, it is ineluctable that my switching to the Democrat party is to take place with immediacy. Let me tell you of all the wonderful reasons for my change.

The Republican Party was founded on the foundation of anti-slavery and fought to free Blacks from slavery before and after the Civil War. President Lincoln had the audacity to sign the Emancipation Proclamation; that is the reason we have these expensive Juneteenth celebrations in our neighborhoods today.

You see, these Republicans caused problems for Democrats, because these people opposed these ideas. So, feeling sorry for the Democrats, I'm switching. But there is more.

Radical, mean-spirited Republicans against the battles of the Democrats would pass the Civil Rights Acts of 1866 and 1875. These acts would give Blacks protection from the Black Codes, which the Southern Democrats worked many long hours to create.

Say it with me: I'm joining the Democrats, because those mean-spirited Republicans took advantage of those Democrats.

Too many historically important Blacks were members of the Republican Party, including Frederick Douglas, Harriet Tubman, Sojourner Truth, Booker T. Washington, and Dr. Martin Luther King, Jr. I feel sorry for the Democrats — they need a little help, because Eisenhower sent U.S. troops to Arkansas to desegregate schools and would create the 1958 Civil Rights Commission.

Adding further pain to the Democrats, this president would appoint Earl Warren to the Supreme Court, leading to the *Brown vs. the Board of Education* decision ending school segregation. Say it with me: I'm joining the Democrats, because those mean-spirited Republicans took advantage of those Democrats.

Republicans held the highest percentage of votes for the passing of the major Civil Rights Acts of the 1960s. Mean-spirited Republicans took advantage of Democrats. I'm switching to be a Democrat, because they need some major help.

Nixon pushed Affirmative Action programs; did you know that James Brown was a Republican and a friend of Nixon's? Anyway, Nixon's plan in 1969 mandated goals and timetables for changes in Philadelphia. This is really taking advantage of Democrats.

President George W. Bush supported spending over $200 million to fight AIDS in Africa, vouchers, faith-based ideas, homeownership and small business ownership, all giving Blacks self-reliance and less dependence on social programs developed by Democrats.

The Democrats were the party of the Ku Klux Klan. I would be crazy not to want to be a member of the Democrat Party knowing this. Democrats used fraud, whips, lynching's and murder in the late 1800s and early 1900s to get the Black vote, passing Black Codes and Jim Crow laws legalizing discrimination.

The founders of the NAACP were Republicans. Say it with me: I'm joining the Democrats, because those mean-spirited Republicans took advantage of those Democrats.

President LBJ, Democrat, called Dr. King the N-word. JFK voted against the 1957 Civil Rights law and opposed the March on Washington. President Clinton refused to comply with a court order mandating shipping companies to develop an Affirmative Action plan.

I can't wait to switch to being a Democrat. Say it with me one more time:

I'm joining the Democrats, because those mean-spirited Republicans took advantage of those Democrats.

No. I'll continue to be a Republican, the party taking advantage of Democrats.

Lucky Rosenbloom welcomes reader responses to 612-661-0923, or email him at l.rosenbloom@yahoo.com

Opinion 3

Racial profiling; or, stupid behavior

Recently, I was the object of racial profiling in Little Canada. It is my desire to share the incident and my response in a letter sent to Sheriff Bob Fletcher, allowing the reader to learn ways of dealing with racial profiling during the incident and its aftermath.

Other options include filing a complaint with the State Department of Human Rights, requesting a meeting with Bob Fletcher and the deputy who profiled me, or ignoring the matter.

You all know me. I will not ignore racial profiling, because this would not be the conservative way. I want you not to miss my next columns because, step by step, you shall witness the process.

To Bob Fletcher, Ramsey County Sheriff's Department:

On October 20, 2007, at 11:31 in the morning, Lucky Rosenbloom was riding his seventeen-thousand-dollar, brand-new Honda Goldwing Motorcycle in Little Canada, looking at some property. Rosenbloom would pass a parked Ramsey County squad car number 6604, with the trunk open, having no Deputy inside.

About 50-100 feet away from the squad, Rosenbloom would pull into the parking lot of the property he was going to look at on Sylvan Street. Rosenbloom was immediately approached by Deputy Dan Eggers, # 290, and asked for identification.

Rosenbloom, being polite, asked the Deputy for PC [Probable Cause] for his questioning. The Deputy offered none, yet continued to ask Rosenbloom for identification. Rosenbloom advised the Deputy that his questioning seemed awkward.

The Deputy, after prodding by Rosenbloom, advised him that he was investigating a report that a person was stealing benches in the area. Now, Rosenbloom was on a motorcycle, making it difficult to transport any picnic-type benches even with Rosenbloom's superior motorcycle skills.

The Deputy, identified as Dan Eggers # 290, would simply walk away, offering no real reason for his stopping Rosenbloom and brief detention. At issue: Whether, if Rosenbloom had walked away, he would have been arrested and, based on 1-2 below, were the Deputy's actions strange? You decide.

Rosenbloom is Black and was in a predominantly White area in Little Canada. No real reason was articulated by the Deputy for his inquiry of Rosenbloom. Was Rosenbloom stealing picnic or any other type of benches on a motorcycle?

So, is this racial profiling or stupid behavior? You decide.

1. The incident was recorded on the squad's system. Will the tape be lost or held for review?

2. The Deputy stated he approached Rosenbloom initially because, while passing his squad, Rosenbloom was looking at it (the squad). With this PC, a lot of Minnesotans can be stopped and questioned.

Signed: Lucky Rosenbloom, a board member of the State Council on Black Minnesotans and chair of the Black Republican Advisory of Minnesota.

Minnesota Nice

I am not being acerbic. Anyone living in Minnesota all of our little lives has been taught, no, indoctrinated into our belief and organized into our social schemes that we live in a liberal state saturated with Democrats loving diversity.

Forget the crap. Why is it that we have all this racism and discrimination at every corner of Minnesota, be it racism in St. Cloud, Duluth, in the Twin Cities, in schools, being watched in stores? I don't get it. This is Minnesota.

The Democrats have Republicans beat 99-1 in Minnesota with smile-in-your-face racism. You heard it here first: Minnesota smile-in-your-face racism. Others may pick up and use my phrase.

Our neighborhoods have been under Democrat control since I was a baby — housing, jobs, racial profiling, equal education and the achievement gap. Are we better off today than we were 20 years ago, even longer, with the control that Democrats have in our community?

Marvin Gaye must have written "What's Goin' On?" for Minnesota smile-in-your-face Democrat racism.

I was a part of a mediation involving a sister working with a bunch of White Hillary Clinton lovers. She reported to work one day only to find the Black dolls that she had proudly placed on her desk with clothing removed and lying on top of each other in sexual positions, one doll having a pin stuck in its butt.

The co-workers, being Bill Clinton lovers, thought it was a joke. I would rather be working around a bunch of President Bush lovers because this way the dolls would have been surrounded by American flags, giving a sense of pride and not sexual degradation of Blacks.

Please stop saying these words

More people, after reading my columns and witnessing my fighting for the rights of the indigent, undereducated, seniors and youth, say, "I wish you were a Democrat."

Spread the word: Stop saying this when you see me. When talking with others, as the words "I wish" comes out, I shall interrupt, saying, "Don't waste your last two words."

Lucky Rosenbloom welcomes reader responses to 612-661-0923, or email him at l.rosenbloom@yahoo.com

Opinion 4

Criminals are one thing, the homeless another

I have no patience for criminals in our community who would sell drugs to our people, crafting drug babies that cannot function in schools and suffer from other illnesses. The police need not make apologies for arresting criminals, including criminals of color who summon fear into the spirits of our elderly who are locked up in the neighborhoods where they have lived and worked all their lives.

Therefore, it bothers me not when others mention the percentage of Blacks in prison. Unlike many of you who are afraid to say this because of the group victimization running through our neighborhood, I say lock them up and get them off the streets.

We pay our police to do a job, and we expect them to do that job with excellence and without apologies for arresting criminals, because the one that is in jail today could be the one that was not allowed to kill a person in your family today.

Our reverence and love ought to go out to the homeless people in the Twin Cities. Let me explain and clarify: The homeless person standing at busy street corners is not selling drugs leading to the devastation of the Black family.

The homeless person is not snatching the purse of some frail elderly woman, or standing in thug-wear in front of your home, or having ugly whores run up and down your block so that you as a woman with no such intent get harassed by sick perverts wanting to find a Community Service Worker (prostitute) and leaving condoms in your yard and/or in front of your home for children to find and play with.

So, the next time you see the homeless person who has made a choice to beg instead of hurting a loved one, instead of wanting to rob, kill, and/or cause you substantial bodily injury, the next time you see a homeless person on a corner with a sign, ask yourself which you would prefer.

Invited to an AA meeting

A friend of mine, knowing that I am Republican and conservative, invited me to go to an AA meeting. After I refused several times, my friend insisted that I was in denial. So, she persuaded this Republican/conservative to go by using some techniques she obviously learned in one of those meetings.

Now, at this meeting it appeared to be some kind of courtesy to allow new members to announce themselves first. I was confused, because my friend advised that all people attending would be like me.

As I looked around, confusion started to saturate my thoughts. It was ineluctable that I would have to speak because all eyes were upon me. I gathered my valor and spoke: "Hello, my name is Lucky and I am African American." Because I was the only person of color attending, I was confused when no one responded with the usual feedback.

This may be the first joke you will read in the year 2007. As the year progresses, I shall create plenty more Lucky jokes.

Black People Anonymous

I am serious — no kidding this time. Here we are in the year 2007. Will one of my readers help me understand the reason that some of us Black people, when gathering at meetings and/or in the workplace, act as if other Blacks don't exist? Come on, this is 2007.

So, being the brother that I am, in these moments I approach Blacks and say, "Wuz up, brother/sister?" While the days are over when it was illegal for more than two Blacks to gather at once, in certain gatherings some of us continue to act like anyone looking Black does not exist.

In these situations, I work the room looking for Blacks, speaking, talking, and attempting to have conversation. Man, one would think my friendly comments were vituperative.

Thus, I am going to start the Twin Cities Black People Anonymous (BPA) group. As the late James Brown would say, "Say it loud, I'm Black and I' am proud."

For this reason, I'll have to find another person to lead the group. Kidding aside, there is a message herein.

Lucky Rosenbloom welcomes reader responses to 612-661-0923, or email him at l.rosenbloom@yahoo.com

Opinion 5

We must drop the victim role to prosper

We must ask ourselves the question, "Why is it that other people from different cultures have achieved substantial economic gains, higher education levels, higher home and business ownership, and more, as compared to African Americans?"

There are three reasons: (1) The federal, state, and local liberal politicians who control our community; (2) Black community leaders who make excuse after excuse for their blunders, and who by doing so have excused our people into becoming victims of blame and doom; and (3) we have failed to give up the acceptance of victimization that is so intensely highly wrought in our culture.

Now, the victim position has failed because we have no real negotiation based within the liberal structure. We are duped into believing that White blame will manifest into business opportunities. The liberals have not and will not let go of White dispensation in our communities. Black leadership must realize that the concept of guilt premeditated at White liberals has a deceptive perception of power, and they (White liberals) have used this guilt game as a way to oppress us economically.

Other cultures not experienced in the guilt game gather themselves collectively to create business and economic opportunity. This independence allows these cultures to thrive. Our leaders have led us into doom while excusing this direction as our being victims.

The new liberal electronic form of discrimination

Young Blacks and one sister in particular, have reported to me that most corporations are now accepting job applications via e-mail/internet. The information goes through a database. The database selects key words for the selected position.

Anyone who makes it through this process is sent an electronic application and could be discriminated against based on one's cultural name, ethnicity, or community. Thus, living over North or in South Minneapolis, or in other areas where negative projections are seen in the liberal media, one could easily be rejected. If you make it to an interview, the job description suddenly changes outside of the required qualifications of your background that initially got you the interview.

One sister believes that she receives calls from potential employers after going through the electronic process, and if a voice message is left on an answering machine with her standard voice mail greeting, a message is left confirming a time for an interview. Once the sister calls back to confirm, this is when liberal discrimination begins. Oh! The name Jill Scottishberg sounds like a Black person.

I want to thank the sister who sent me this response. These are the new and perhaps most hidden and protected forms of liberal discrimination into the next century, and Black civil rights organizations don't know how to deal with this sophisticated racism because it is camouflaged using electronic technology.

President Clinton educated the liberal racist

The cool brother Clinton, the "first Black president," in his 1997 inaugural speech asked over one million college folks to read to America's children. Slick Clinton was using a well-known Democrat paradigm of redemptive liberalism to create White power by establishing the Black reading problem as a stipulation that implied that the White liberal teacher is hope for the poor student. This was a slick way of fostering the myth of affirmative action, which is often seen as a way to help the marginal Black.

Mayor Rybak responds to White liberal deaths

Since the Iraq War began, we have had 30 Minnesotans killed serving our country. Since 2001, we have had 224 homicides in Minneapolis. Two were White and killed in business areas at the hands of criminals of color.

Where are the Black leaders to challenge Rybak, to have discourse about his loud action for more police and resources when people of color are killing people of color? The liberal mayor has demonstrated redemptive racism, yet no Black leader made a serious issue of this inept action. Why? Because they are wearing min-skirts and hot pants and are afraid to speak out for fear of losing any crumbs given in the past to keep the Black warriors from becoming conservative.

In 2004, the violent crime rate for Minneapolis was more than two and a half times the national average. The murder rate for the nation was 5.5 per 100, 0000. The Luckster does not claim to be an expert, or even good in math, but this means that the Minneapolis rate was almost three times the national average, 14.1 per 100,000.

The FBI statistics indicate an increase in crime in Murderapo— I mean, Minneapolis. Crime across the nation decreased while crime here increased. Mayor Rybak, where were you before the 2006 uptown and Block E killings? All of these crimes occur under the liberal DFL-controlled community.

My book is on the way

I am writing a book that we hope to have published within one year entitled *Liberal Racism that Creates the Black Conservative*, the writings of Lucky Rosenbloom. This book will take a serious look at racism in our communities and how the next generation of young Blacks will respond.

I would like to offer a personal appreciation to the sister who shared her experience of liberal racism for this column. If you have an experience to share, call and/or email us.

Lucky Rosenbloom welcomes reader responses to 612-661-0923, or email him at l.rosenbloom@yahoo.com

Pullquote: We are duped into believing that White blame will manifest into business opportunities.

Opinion 6

Liberal policies very dangerous to your health

I'm not ignoring anything.

I exercise, run about 15 miles each week, lift weights, pop 80 pushups in one minute, and work to build muscular strength and muscular endurance. So, I'm not ignoring anything.

This Black Conservative will not ignore chest pains. No, not the Luckster. If I ever have chest pain that feels like 30 liberals sat on my chest, you best believe that the Luckster is going to save money and hold down future costs by going to the closest emergency room.

Hearing liberals beg all the time can cause a conservative like me pain in my left arm, and after many attempts to talk sense into a liberal with added pain in my jaw, matched with sweating and shortness of breath, well, you can be assured the Luckster is headed to the emergency room. This is a sign that liberal policies are giving me a heart attack.

This Black Conservative is not ignoring shortness of breath. Man, I listened to a recent Democrat presidential debate. None of those clowns answered questions with substance. The irony of it all could cause anyone to have walked at least one block, or to have run downstairs for some juice and back up the stairs to continue listening.

If I experience shortness of breath after this kind of movement, motivated by liberals whose only real answer to any question about programs is taking money out of our pockets to support absurd ideas, the Luckster is not going to ignore this. I'm going to see a conservative doctor.

Watching Hillary Clinton talk about ending the war in Iraq, yet voting to fund the war, makes me want to choke. Listening to Hillary Clinton makes me so sick, I, don't want to eat. However, if my pants no longer fit thanks to junk food, the Luckster is going to a conservative doctor, because listening to Hillary may have caused me to develop cancer.

A lot of what liberals say is a bunch of crap (I substituted crap for the desired word). It would be nice if we could just eat up liberal policies for digesting and flushing. However, their policies are worse than any food poisoning.

So, if their policies digest with blood in my urine, or stool, you got it — I'm going to see a conservative doctor. You must understand that it's not my desire to look at digested liberal waste, but it's integral to my health to do exactly that from time to time after eating liberal policies.

Let me stick with this urination of liberal policies. Let's say that liberal policies have been so damaging to Black people that I had to put their policies in a blender with a bottle of Gatorade and drink their policies in order to prevent further harm to Black people. Taking this risk because of my care for you, the reader, well, let's say that this would cause changes in my urination pattern.

I am getting up too many times at night to pi#@ liberal policies. I have accomplished my goal of weakening liberal policies, but now my urination looks weak also, and it's difficult to get my urination started. See, it's possible that liberal policies have given the Luckster prostate cancer.

I will not ignore these symptoms. Say it with me: I'm going to see a conservative doctor.

This has to work. It's time to get the Minnesota Democrat platform. Once in my possession, I'll kick it all up and down the halls of the local DFL, the halls of the city council that is doing nothing about the newly created jobs with respect to the bridge collapse.

Why are Blacks fighting for these jobs? Don't blame this on Pawlenty.

If the Luckster has any leg swelling or accumulation of fluid in my ankles or feet, that means kicking these policies may have caused heart, kidney or liver disease. Say it with me once again: I'm going to see a conservative doctor.

Liberal policies make my skin itch. Sometimes, reading liberal policies, hearing liberals speak, and hearing liberal doomsday preachers cause skin lesions. If these liberal policy lesions fail to heal after a few days — get this — those liberal policies and speakers have ruined my circulation and given me diabetes or skin cancer.

If those liberal policy wounds become larger or change color and shape, say it with me one last time: I'm going to see a conservative doctor.

There is a message here for Black men. We like to stay away from physicians until it's too late. Don't ignore warning signs that liberal policies have affected your health. As soon as you experience any of the signs expressed herein, go and see a conservative doctor, because liberal prescriptions will not work. However, this could be a good malpractice suit.

Women, there is a message in this column for you also.

Lucky Rosenbloom welcomes reader responses to 612-661-0923, or email him at l.rosenbloom@yahoo.com

Pullquote: Sometimes, reading liberal policies, hearing liberals speak, and hearing liberal doomsday preachers cause skin lesions.

Opinion 7

Coming to a liberal city near you:
the New Black American Political Machine

Democrats' liberal policies keep people dependent using social policies so heavy to lift during your bench press that these liberal policies create and hold you down in poverty. The heavy weights of welfare make it difficult for Black liberals to lift themselves into capitalism because of too much governmental regulation designed to prevent Blacks from starting businesses, which establish self-reliance and responsibility for our families.

Liberal policies such as welfare and other handouts keep Blacks weighted down in water, never to surface, while suffering the spiritual death of waiting, begging, and keeping hope alive in a liberal system of high taxes. Liberals working their way out of this liberal bondage of dependency into self-reliance are forced to pay high taxes supporting welfare and other handout programs, limiting the food on your tables and taxing you out of your homes and other ownership investments.

Those of you reading my column know much of what is said is the truth. How many of you, after obtaining higher education and landing that good job, at one time were accepting of liberal polices but now is upset because of the money coming out of your checks to support welfare and other liberal policies?

Come on — many of you can now be heard saying those favorite words, "I am tired of all this money coming out of my check for people on welfare." Remember, you could at one time have been one of those people. An education, a job, home ownership, having a business and paying high taxes year after year makes one a conservative real fast.

What really scares a liberal is when one sees a Black parent heavily involved in their child's education, because the liberal must see him/herself as the great White teaching hope. Liberals do not like seeing Black parents involved in their schools, because this means more control those parents have over curriculum, the teacher unions, accountability and measured outcomes.

You can see the panic if each one of you told 10 other Black parents, and they told 10 other Black parents, that on the first and last Tuesday of each month we are all going to spend two hours in any given school. Wow!

Black parents in schools just two days each month would drive liberal teachers crazy who are doing nothing but collecting a paycheck. Organize in your child's school, and make this happen now.

We should have a major movement in our community advising young people to prepare for the jobs of the 21st century. If a Black teen put as much time into his/her books, reading, math and social studies as they do smoking weed, playing basketball, hanging out on the street looking cool and waiting to be MVP of his home play station, our community would turn out wondrous scholars.

Out of high school, I joined the military. With the discipline I already had on entering, matched with the drive and never-give-up attitude learned from the military and my parents, I was prepared to improvise, overcome and adapt to working and pursuing education, meeting the mandate of any given societal change.

Having the mindset of a dependent liberal would have destroyed my entire character, and we witness this destruction of our youth today. They are not victims of being ghettoized, but rather of being liberalized into failure.

Liberal policies have caused destruction in the Black family system. From the acceptance of gay marriage to moving prayer out of schools, these policies have all taken away from the traditional Black family and God as our endurance. We see HIV, gays, all embarrassments to the Black family, and all because of liberal policies that Black preachers will not denounce in their pulpits because of being more committed to the Democrats than the word of God.

Black liberals have allowed our people to enter into a steady course of Willie Lynch self-destruction by accepting the liberal message that gay is fine, anti-God and anti-Black values being God, family and moral values. We must repent, turn away from this evilness, and reclaim our family values.

The New Black American Political Machine must give up the liberal policies of self-destruction and work for lower taxes, calling for liberals not to penalize earnings and investments; calling on government to create a transparent and accountable budget; privatizing public services; capping taxes and expenditures; funding our students and not failing neighborhood schools;

reforming Medicaid programs; reforming Welfare; and protecting employees from the politics of unions and racism.

This is the New Black Movement. Organize and start this movement in your areas today. Make it happen. The shorties will be glad you did.

Minneapolis Civil Rights Commission

Why are so many liberals afraid of Michael Jordan and Ron Brandon? Ninety-nine percent of the perpetrators of racism and discrimination in the city of Minneapolis are Democrats. If I were such a Democrat, I wouldn't want our two unafraid brothers around.

Onward!

Lucky Rosenbloom welcomes reader responses to 612-661-0923, or email him at l.rosenbloom@yahoo.com

Opinion 8

State takes blood samples of newborn Black babies

by Lucky Rosenbloom

Minnesota Spokesman-Recorder

Originally posted 5/28/2008

Are you aware that the State of Minnesota has been amassing newborn baby blood samples for over 10 years? Now, no doubt, the majority of these samples are taken from children of color.

It's true. Unbeknownst to most parents, the Minnesota Department of Health has warehoused DNA information on over 780,000 infants since 1997. If you live in the Black community, do you know how to find out if your baby's sample was taken?

In 2006, the state legislature passed a genetic privacy law requiring expressed written patient consent prior to gathering genetic information. Republicans moved this bill into law because we had serious concerns with privacy and notification rights.

But, instead of complying with the law, the Department of Health continued its practice collecting newborn DNA without a parent's written authorization. Black parents must be outraged at this, because it is my claim that most samples were taken from urban hospitals.

This is an issue that leaders in the Black community, the Black pastors, should be delivering from their pulpits. Ask your community leader, your pastor, why they are not speaking out about this possible profiling.

Last year, a Minnesota judge ordered the Department of Health to cease its illegal activity. But, the Health Department ignored the judge's ruling and instead vigorously worked to change the law in order to exempt infants from Minnesota's genetic privacy law.

I'll ask again: Why are the pastors and/or leaders not bringing this matter to public light? I'll answer: Because liberals are violating our newborn children and because liberals control some of our leaders and some of our churches. Only a Black conservative can bring this matter into "Issues and New Perspectives."

The state legislature has caved in to the demands of the Department of Health and passed bill number S.F. 3138, which eliminates the requirement for a parent to opt-in to the collection process. Call your Senate member and ask how he or she voted on this issue. Better yet, do some homework and discover the number of Democrats voting to violate your newly born children in our community.

Under the new law, the Department of Health will be able to collect an infant's DNA unless a parent expressly opts out of the process within 24 hours. Understand: If a Black parent is unaware of the option, or worse, if the Black parent does not know about this taking of blood samples, violation will occur.

I am telling you that most samples are taken from Black babies. While the law requires a parental disclosure, reading a disclosure and signing an opt-out form will be the last thing on the mind of the parents within the first 24 hours after the birth of a child, because Black mothers/fathers are more concerned about getting the child through the first 24 hours alive and healthy. Also, many parents of color from other countries are afraid to challenge White staff in hospitals.

This is abusive and one of the most racist acts within the medical profession since the Tuskegee experiments. This brings liberal racism in Minnesota to a new high of evilness. Bottom line, this bill reduces a patient's right to privacy by changing the law from an opt-in to an opt-out process. It puts thousands of individuals at risk of having their private genetic information inappropriately used by the state without their knowledge or consent.

Governor Pawlenty is now the only person who can prevent this bill from becoming law, and you must let your voices be heard. Tell liberals no.

Educate yourself today by studying at the following web location: http://www.minnesotamajority.org/Home/tabid/112/EntryID/78/Default.aspx. Forward this message to your friends and sisters having babies as of 2006. Ask them to take action as well.

Join me at the Council on Black Minnesotans Government Liaison Committee by calling 612-661-0923. We can organize and work as a team of New Black Americans to stop this racist practice.

Update: Pawlenty vetoes 'DNA Warehouse' Bill

In a letter dated May 20, 2008, Governor Tim Pawlenty writes that he has vetoed S.F. 3138, the genetic information and DNA bill. S.F. 3138 would have eliminated current informed parent consent requirements for government storage, use, and dissemination of newborn citizen blood and DNA.

As chair of the State Council on Black Minnesotans Government Liaison Committee, I have delivered a letter to the Minnesota Department of Health to immediately comply with the genetic privacy law consent requirements.

Lucky Rosenbloom welcomes reader responses to 612-661-0923, or email him at l.rosenbloom@yahoo.com

Opinion 9

Leadership – Theory & Practice

A Man Not Afraid to Lead

Let me start off by stating, I am critical of labeling a person a leader due to the fact leaders in my opinion must boldly act daily in the definition of that which they are labeled. Often leaders are not that, but in this case Mr. Lucky Rosenbloom (yes Lucky is his birth name) is that and then some. Mr. Rosenbloom is a leader in my opinion who exhibits that which he persistently aims to develop and unleash in supporters and non-supporters alike. He is an individual that influences other individuals to achieve common goals by collectively working together utilizing their talents and intellect. In his own words "I am not a leader, I am someone who has found a way to communicate to others about issues we all have in common and aid everyone to move it through" (personal communication, February 21st, 2008). He protests he does not have followers, but supporters, wherefore he is voice piece for the aggressive and passive supporters he represents. In *Secrets of Attila the Hun*, leaders have to want to be in charge, because those are the chieftains who are different from another; who is possess the willingness to serve, yet distinguishable by their wisdom, sincerity, benevolence, authority and courage.

Nonetheless, Mr. Rosenbloom was a compassionate emergent leader way before he was an appointed or assigned leader.

In like manner, Mr. Rosenbloom too exemplified the leadership practice of psychodynamic approach, whereas he embodies various personality types with a main one of course that does not match those of his followers or in his own words supporters. He has various supporters' idiosyncrasies and his own personality quirks and characteristics to work with and for those that might not have come forward to act on a common goal if he had not. Mr. Rosenbloom credits his mother and father for the strong leadership qualities that they modeled and instilled in him from a very young age. The psychodynamic approach avouches paternal influence as a major premise, which too is often a metaphor resembled in corporations and other organizations alike.

Furthermore, Mr. Rosenbloom authenticates another personality characteristic depicted by Mr. Maccoby of the productive narcissist that does not aim to impress, but takes pride in his accomplishments along with being humorous, which is often self-directed. Egoism and narcissism are two different descriptors that may be mistaken for the other, whereby egoism is a self – centered mode of thinking that aim to impress. Indeed Mr. Rosenbloom is a live comic act everyday that pokes fun of him in addition to others while simultaneously cultivating the masses to extend their minds to new horizons of thought. His humor and stimulating perspective is resonated throughout his book, *Liberal Racism Creates the Black Conservative* and his commentary column in the St. Paul Spokesman Recorder. The productive narcissist leader is one that is a visionary, wherefore Mr. Rosenbloom undoubtedly is such a visionary as the President of the Black Conservative Committee of Minnesota and Chair of the Black Republican Coalition not to mention an entrepreneur of several businesses. As Mr. Rosenbloom meekly told me, "lead in a way that your vision eventually becomes your supporter's vision".

At any rate, Mr. Rosenbloom actively lead for positive change by persuading Sen. Norm Coleman and other political officials to dedicate an area in our Nation's Capitol titled, "Emancipation Hall" in recognition of Slave Laborers who helped to build it. This is an honor to not only Black people, but also all American people. Then for the recognition to take place during Black History month is a testimony to the greatness of Americans in politics willing to correct the wrongs of history. This is the type of transformational/ transactional leadership that all leaders should be manifesting to make our world a better place.

Mr. Rosenbloom completed the Myers-Briggs typology survey in the Leadership and Practice book, page 261; his psychological type resulted as ESTJ that is a value of organization and a methodical, focused, and planned appearance. Hence, his leadership personality encompasses personal power, meaning referent and expert power in addition to organizational power that promote future leadership qualities in others and future activities; moreover constituting his preference of personality function as a thinker and a feeler. This thinker and feeler model which he possess as he facilitates and organizes empowerment forums with a panel of influential political and community people for high school boys and girls encouraging them to be active, objective, and empathic problem solvers as the new age leaders they are called to be.

To conclude Mr. Rosenbloom is a leader who clearly leads by example with such tenacity that is contagiously inspiring. He is one who empathetically understands human nature, which enables him to be a decisive negotiator whereas he is charged with enthusiasm to lead in making positive changes for the greater good of us all.

Lucky Rosenbloom welcomes reader responses to 612-661-0923, or email him at l.rosenbloom@yahoo.com

Opinion 10

The New Council on Black Minnesotans

Our community has a new group of Black professionals serving as Board Members having diverse Backgrounds and experiences that will revitalize the COBM, into a respected, honorable and highly recognized state entity representing and advocating towards improved standards of living for Blacks in our great State of Minnesota.

I have to give adulation to the governor's staff for selecting such a fine group of Blacks to serve as Board Members. I expect these new Board Members to be the best Board ever. Without any doubt, these new members are the most creative, educated in intellectual group of people ever to serve as Board Members.

I recorded one the COBM, Board meetings of May 2008. I will give you a free copy of the tape. Witness the professionalism of these new members' debate, have dichotomy discourse, come to a conclusion, followed by direct action. I am telling you. These new members will not be toyed with at all.

The results of the coming

Audit will not be at the responsibility of these new members. However, should the audit findings be as poor as previous audits under previous Board Members over the years, I have no doubt that these new Board members shall act accordingly.

Remember. You heard it from this columnist first. The Council on Black Minnesotans, under the leadership of these new, young, exciting, talented, undaunted, innovative, progressive, and diverse with respect to ideas, yet, cohesiveness, will bring, revitalization the COBM. Our community is in for a long over-due treat of high-standard representation.

The information below is to both educate and to have you hold the Board accountable. These New Board Members desire and expect our people to hold each of them, including myself, as Chair of the COBM, Government Liaison Committee accountable to our charge.

Subd. 3. Duties. The council shall:

(a) advise the governor and the legislature on the nature of the issues confronting Black people in this state;
(b) advise the governor and the legislature on statutes or rules necessary to ensure that Black people have access to benefits and services provided to people in this state;
(c) recommend to the governor and the legislature any revisions in the state's affirmative action program and other steps that are necessary to eliminate underutilization of Blacks in the state's work force;
(d) recommend to the governor and the legislature legislation to improve the economic and social condition of Black people in this state;
(e) serve as a conduit to state government for organizations of Black people in the state;
(f) serve as a referral agency to assist Black people to secure access to state agencies and programs;
(g) serve as a liaison with the federal government, local government units, and private organizations on matters relating to the Black people of this state;
(h) perform or contract for the performance of studies designed to suggest solutions to problems of Black people in the areas of education, employment, human rights, health, housing, social welfare, and other related areas;
(i) implement programs designed to solve problems of Black people when authorized by other statute, rule, or order;
(j) review data provided by the commissioner of human services under section 260C.215, subdivision 5, and present recommendations on the out-of-home placement of Black children. Recommendations must be presented to the commissioner and the legislature by February 1, 1990; November 1, 1990; and November 1 of each year thereafter; and
(k) publicize the accomplishments of Black people and their contributions to this state.

The Council on Black Minnesotans is a part of the State of Minnesota's governor's administration with the above-duties supported by Minnesota laws. You, the reader, ought to organize and develop such a Black legislative entity in your State, as well.

With this type of Council in Minnesota, why, did a group of liberal

Democrats in the legislature attempt to shut it down? This has to get one thinking about racism alive, liberal style.

Opinion 11

Lucky in the Court

I, having the ability to do so, because of being conservative, meaning one does not accept the victim role of inability, represented myself in a Personal Injury lawsuit against a big law firm with attachments to one major American Family Insurance.

Now, previous to the Deposition you are about to read, I filed a Motion for Partial Summary Judgment to Stipulate liability. The big shot lawyer wanted nothing to do with this. However, after the Deposition, the big shot lawyer would change this tone and Stipulate to liability.

Keep in mind, insurance companies spend millions in an effort to paint a picture in society that people are faking injuries. This is designed to make you take small meaningless settlements. Knowing this and being a Republican, a fighter, I filed a lawsuit to show all Minnesotans that they must stand strong when suffering from injuries because of the negligence of others, whereby, you and/or others are hurt. Read the actual Deposition of one non-trained citizen, against a big lawyer in a big firm. Witness the Defendant being caught in a lie.

1

STATE OF MINNESOTA DISTRICT COURT
COUNTY OF HENNEPIN FOURTH JUDICIAL DISTRICT
———————————————————————
Mr. Lucky Rosenbloom,
Plaintiff,
vs. Court File No. 27-CV-07-26620
Richard Leo Hanft,
Defendant.
———————————————————————
DEPOSITION
The following is the deposition of

RICHARD LEO HANFT, taken before Kelly E. Kohls, Court Reporter, Notary Public, pursuant to Notice of Taking Deposition, at the Offices of Depo International, 1330 Jersey Street, Suite 200, Minneapolis, Minnesota, commencing at approximately 11:38 a.m., April 30th, 2008.

APPEARANCES:

Plaintiff appeared Pro Se:

Maryland Lucky Rosenbloom
1370 Coach Road
#209
Saint Paul, Minnesota 55108
(612) 661-0923

On Behalf of the Defendant:
Brian D. Stofferahn, Esquire
ATTORNEY AT LAW
6131 Blue Circle Drive
Minneapolis, Minnesota 55343-9130
(952) 224-5959
bstoffer@amfam.com

DEPOSITION REFERENCE INDEX

EXAMINATION

By Mr. Rosenbloom: 4

OBJECTIONS

By Mr. Stofferahn: 6, 7, 12, 13, 17, 24, 25, 30, 31

EXHIBIT INDEX

EXHIBIT A MARKED, Document Certification Letter from the Minnesota Department of Public Safety and a Driver License Jacket Inquiry Record Request................................14

EXHIBIT B MARKED, Handwritten Diagram Drawn by Richard Hanft.................................23

EXHIBIT C MARKED, Order............................28

P R O C E E D I N G S

Whereupon, the deposition of RICHARD LEO HANFT was commenced at 11:38 a.m. as follows:

RICHARD LEO HANFT,
after having been first duly sworn,
deposes and says under oath as follows:

***

EXAMINATION

BY MR. ROSENBLOOM:

Q. My name is Maryland Lucky Rosenbloom. I'm a Pro Se litigant. I'm going to be asking you a series of questions about an accident that happened. I'm going to ask some information bout your background. If you do not understand any question for whatever reason, please let me know. If you do not, I will have to assume that you understand the question. If you're not sure of the answer to a question, do not guess. If you need to take a break at any reason at all — for any reason at all, just let me know, and we'll take a break.

It's important that you respond verbally for the stenographer. She can only type what you say. She cannot interpret shrugs, nods, or jesters. She has to take down every word to make sure that the record is complete. Assume that I am blind and cannot see whatever it is that you are showing me. Describe everything in as much detail as you can.

Please allow me to finish my questions before you answer them. The court reporter can only take down what you say, she cannot take down what two people are saying at the same time. Also, by letting me finish my question, you will know exactly what I'm asking. I know that in a normal conversation we will probably finish each other's sentences, because we know where the other person is likely going. However, here we need to be courteous to the court reporter so that she

can make an accurate record of what is being said. At the end of this statement or deposition a transcript will be made available for your attorney and for yourself to look over to make any adjustments that you may deem necessary. Do you understand what I have said?
A. Yes, I do.
Q. Okay. Would you please state and spell your full name for the record.
A. Okay. Richard Leo Hanft, R-i-c-h-a-r-d, L-e-o, H-a-n-f, as in Frank, t, as in Tom.

Q. What is your date of birth?
A. June 18th, 1953.
Q. And your present address?
A. 16011 Pierce Street Northeast, Ham Lake, Minnesota, 55304.
Q. Was this your address at the time of the accident?
A. Yes, it was.
Q. Does anyone live with you there?
A. My wife.
Q. And please provide the name of your wife.
A. Sure. Donna Jean, same last name, Hanft.
Q. And what is your wife's date of birth?
A. March 8th, 1955.
Q. And what is your Social Security number?
MR. STOFFERAHN: I'm going to object as not reasonably calculated to lead to admissible evidence.
MR. ROSENBLOOM: Your objection is noted.
BY MR. ROSENBLOOM:
Q. Answer the question.

MR. STOFFERAHN: Sir, I'm not done with my objection yet.
MR. ROSENBLOOM: Complete your objection.
MR. STOFFERAHN: It's not reasonably calculated to lead to admissible evidence, and it's outside the scope of discovery, and based upon that, I'm going to instruct my client not to answer.
MR. ROSENBLOOM: Your objection has been noted.
BY MR. ROSENBLOOM:
Q. You will answer the question.
MR. STOFFERAHN: No, he doesn't have to answer the question. I've instructed him not to.
MR. ROSENBLOOM: Then why don't we have a call with the judge, a conference call. You know the rules of the deposition as well as I do.
MR. STOFFERAHN: I do.
MR. ROSENBLOOM: Okay. Then we will come back to that question, and we'll get the judge to make a decision on that question. So we will come back to that question, if there's time. We'll just get through some of the other ones.
BY MR. ROSENBLOOM:
Q. Are you employed right now?

A. Yes, I am.
Q. Where are you employed?
A. Arby's/Sbarro.
Q. And what's the location?
A. Okay. It's 120 Southwest 12th Street, Forest Lake, Minnesota, 55025.
Q. Were you employed at the time of the accident?
A. Yes, I was.
Q. And were you employed at the same location?
A. Yes, I was.
Q. And I see you wear eyeglasses?
A. Yes, I do.

Q. How long have you had a driver's
license?
A. Since about 19 — Let's see. About 19
— I'm just thinking, about 1969, roughly,
approximately. I — Yeah. I might be a year off or
so.
Q. And you've had that, your license in
Minnesota since that time?
A. No.
Q. Let me rephrase the question. How long
have you had a driver's license in the State of

Minnesota?
A. Since 1971.
Q. And did you take a driver's ed course?
A. In Minnesota or where I —
Q. In Minnesota.
A. In Minnesota, no.
Q. Have you taken any driver's ed courses
in any other states?
A. Yes.
Q. What state was that?
A. Illinois.
Q. How long ago was that?
A. Well, that was 1969, roughly, prior to
me getting my license in Illinois.
Q. Please tell me, do you remember the
date of the accident?
A. January — The first part of January.
I — I don't remember the exact date.
Q. What day of the week was it?
A. Oh, it was a Monday.
Q. A Monday?
A. Yes.
Q. Okay. Where were you going at the
time?
A. Well, at the time I was heading — At

10

the time I was heading — I was going to be going home.

Q. Okay. You were going home. Were you late —

A. Was I late?

Q. — going home?

A. No.

Q. Where were you coming from at the time?

A. Well, Little Canada.

Q. Okay. And was anyone with you in the vehicle?

A. No.

Q. So let me get this clear. You were coming from Little Canada in South Minneapolis. My question is, you were in South Minneapolis, where were you going?

A. Okay. I was going to visit my sons, okay, but that went on the back burner, I mean, when I had the accident.

Q. Okay. Please tell me what make and model the vehicle that you were driving that day of the accident?

A. Okay. 1996 Nissan Maxima.

Q. Two-door, four-door?

A. It's a four-door.

11

Q. And the color of the vehicle?

A. The color is beige.

Q. Okay. Were you on any medication at the time?

A. No, I was not on any medication.

Q. Are you on any medication now?

A. No, I'm not on any medication now.

Q. Going back to the day of the accident —

A. Uh-huh.

Q. — could you see the road, was it — what was the visibility like?

A. The pavement was dry and —

Q. Visibility.

A. Yeah, it was dry, so it wasn't — there was no — it wasn't — there was no snow coming down or anything. It was —

Q. Okay. Has your insurance — What was the amount of damage done to your vehicle?

A. I believe it was approximately — I can't swear exactly, but approximately $2,000.

Q. And describe to me, excuse me, what happened the day of the accident. Give me the details. What happened, as you remember it?

A. Okay. As I remember, you were stopped

12

ahead of me, and I was unable to stop in time, which I should have, but, and I hit your trailer hitch that extended out from it, and that's what did the damage to my vehicle.

Q. So did you attempt to apply your brakes? Was there any skidding?

A. Oh, definitely, I tried applying my brakes. Was there skidding? For a very, probably a very short distance.

Q. And what caused the accident, do you think? Why did you not see my vehicle? Well, you said it was stopped, so obviously you saw the vehicle, it was stopped, is that your testimony?

A. Your vehicle appeared to be stopped, yes.

Q. And when you exited the vehicle, you told me you were daydreaming; is that correct?

A. I don't — Yeah, I don't recall saying that.

Q. You don't recall you said you were daydreaming?

A. I don't recall that, no.

Q. Have you been in any other accidents in the last ten years?

MR. STOFFERAHN: I'm going to object.

13

Not reasonably calculated to lead to admissible evidence, and instruct him not to answer.
MR. ROSENBLOOM: We'll come back to that question when we call the judge.
BY MR. ROSENBLOOM:
Q. Have you had any moving violations in the last ten years?
MR. STOFFERAHN: Same objection, same instruction.
BY MR. ROSENBLOOM:
Q. Have you had any moving violations since the accident?
MR. STOFFERAHN: You can answer that.
THE WITNESS: Moving violations since the accident? No, no moving violations since the accident.
BY MR. ROSENBLOOM:
Q. Okay. Have you — So you haven't had any moving violations since the accident?
A. No.
Q. Have you been in any accidents since the accident, not before, but since the accident?
A. Okay. Since the accident, I was in an accident, yes.
Q. And tell me about that accident. What

14

day was that accident on?
A. It was at the Anoka post office, and a person in a truck backed into me, okay, and his insurance company paid for the repair of my vehicle.
Q. Okay. So it's your testimony that you have not had any moving violations? Have you been given any tickets, any citations since the accident?
A. No, I have not.
Q. Okay. So it's your testimony you haven't had any moving violations, you haven't been given any citations since the accident?

A. That's correct.

MR. ROSENBLOOM: I would like to introduce what I'm going to mark as Exhibit A.

(Whereupon, Deposition Exhibit A was marked for identification.)

MR. ROSENBLOOM: I would like to describe what has been marked as Exhibit A as a Document Certification Letter from the Minnesota Department of Public Safety. Would you care to look at this document?

MR. STOFFERAHN: Well, if you're going to ask him questions about it, I need to see it.

BY MR. ROSENBLOOM:

Q. I would like to say what's been marked

15

as Exhibit A is a Document Certification Letter from the Minnesota Department of Public Safety, which is a driving record that I've pulled I believe to be on Richard Leo Hanft, with the address of 16011 Pierce Street Northeast, in Ham Lake, where it appears that on 06-11, 2007, which would be after the accident —

A. Okay.

Q. — according to this, you were, in fact, given a ticket or a citation, it looks like, for illegal or improper use of lane. Would you like to see that?

A. I see it.

Q. Is that true, were you given a ticket for improper use, as it states on the —

A. That is true.

Q. So your testimony earlier that you had not received any citations for any type of violations since the accident, that's not true, is it?

A. That's correct.

Q. Now, you are under oath, you realize that?

A. Yes. I — I realize that.

Q. Let me ask you another question. Have you seen a copy of the Summons and Complaint with regards to this motor vehicle accident?

16

A. I don't understand.

Q. Let me rephrase the question. You were served with a Summons and Complaint; is that correct?

A. Are you referring to a ticket or?

Q. Okay. Let me rephrase the question.

A. I'm sorry. I don't — Okay.

Q. We're finished with this part for now, referring to the document.

A. Okay. Okay. We're finished.

Q. My question now is, you — my process server served you with a copy of the Summons and Complaint relevant to this court case.

A. Okay. That's correct.

Q. That's correct. How many times did he serve you?

A. Once.

Q. So if he, my process server, has an Affidavit saying that you were served twice, are you saying that would be inaccurate?

A. That would be inaccurate, because I was served once.

Q. Is there anyone else living in your home, besides yourself and your wife?

A. No, there's nobody else in my home.

Q. So it's your testimony before this

17

court today — or before this deposition today, that you saw my vehicle stopped; is that correct?

A. Yes, that's correct.

Q. And you — It was stopped — To the best of your knowledge, my vehicle was stopped. Was I waiting for a stoplight?

A. You were stopped, it must be for a stoplight, yes.

Q. And it's your testimony, my vehicle was

stopped, I was waiting for a stoplight, the light was
read, is that your testimony?
A. I believe the light was red.
Q. And is your testimony to this court
that for whatever the reason was, daydreaming or
whatever the reasons, it's your testimony for this
deposition today that you, in fact, slammed into the
back of my motor vehicle because you were unable to
stop?
MR. STOFFERAHN: I'm going to object to
the form of the question.
MR. ROSENBLOOM: I'll rephrase.
BY MR. ROSENBLOOM:
Q. It's your testimony here today that you
did run into the back of my vehicle?
A. I did run into the back of your

18

vehicle.
Q. And the road was clear?
A. The road was dry, yes.
Q. The road was dry, I'm sorry. And it
was a clear day?
A. Yes.
Q. And it was $2,000 of damage done to
your vehicle, according to your testimony?
A. Approximately, yes.
Q. How did you leave the scene that day?
A. I drove away.
Q. You were driving a car?
A. Yes.
Q. Did your car — Did damage to your
vehicle, did that include radiator damage?
A. Yes, it did.
Q. And, in fact, there was radiator fluid
on the ground that day; isn't that correct?
A. There was some radiator fluid on the
ground, that's correct.
Q. So in light of your testimony —
MR. STOFFERAHN: Excuse me, would you

wait until he's completely done with his answer.
MR. ROSENBLOOM: Sure, sure. I don't have a problem. Thank you for reminding me to do

19

that.
BY MR. ROSENBLOOM:
Q. What was your answer to the question?
A. Yes, there was some radiator fluid on the ground.
Q. Some radiator fluid on the ground. And in light of your testimony regarding the illegal or improper use of lane change, which seems to be contradicting your testimony today, you are telling me today that with radiator fluid on the ground, and the damage to your vehicle, and if I remember that day, your vehicle, the radiator fluid, your vehicle was steaming; is that correct?
A. It was — I believe you're right, correct, as far as it was starting to steam —
Q. Starting —
A. — and I turned it off, right.
Q. Starting to steam?
A. Right.
Q. And did you drive your car back to Ham Lake or to a relatives house?
A. No. I drove it to Heritage Auto Body.
Q. And how far was that from the accident site?
A. I don't know exactly.

20

Q. Two miles, three miles?
A. No. It was more than 2 or 3 miles. It was over 10 miles.
Q. And is that — What's the location of that entity?
A. It's — I can't tell you the exact address, but it's on Coon Rapids Boulevard —

Q. Coon Rapids Boulevard?
A. — in Coon Rapids.
Q. And when you took your car to that
entity, did you leave it for repairs, or did you drive
it home?
A. No, I left it there.
Q. You left it there?
A. I left it there.
Q. And did you leave it there under the
advice of the owners or the people that you took it
to, or was that —
A. No. They —
Q. — your own decision to leave it there?
A. Yeah, that was my decision. They were
already closed for the day, but — yeah, they were
already closed for the day.
Q. Okay. So, and you left the vehicle
there. How did you get home?

21

A. My wife picked me up.
Q. Do you recall where the accident
happened, what street it was on?
A. Just before Bloomington, on 31st.
Q. When — Now, I'm going to refer to
myself as plaintiff, so when I say plaintiff,
understand I'm referring to myself. When did you
first see the plaintiff's vehicle the day of the
accident? When did you first see the plaintiff's
vehicle?
A. Probably shortly before I hit it.
Q. And what was the first thing you saw?
A. Your truck, your vehicle.
Q. And you've already testified that my
vehicle was stopped?
A. Yes, I did.
Q. What was the other traffic doing around
you, do you remember?
A. Well, it was moving, it was moving. I
mean, there was traffic going the other way. It was

moving.
Q. Uh-huh. Did you sound your horn?
A. No, I did not.
Q. Did you warn the plaintiff in any way that you were about to hit the plaintiff's vehicle,

22

meaning myself?
A. No, I did not.
Q. And explain, you said you attempted to stop, but explain that. Exactly what did you do in your attempt to stop?
A. Okay. When I saw your vehicle, I hit my brakes hard, and I almost stopped, but I didn't stop in time.
Q. Okay. I'm going to ask you to please draw a picture of the accident, showing your car, my car, being the plaintiff's car, and any other cars around you. I'll give you the back of here, if you'd like.
A. It might take me a little bit of time.
Q. Just to the best of your ability, that's okay.
A. Okay. So I'll make the street. (The witness indicated.)
MR. STOFFERAHN: Let me see it before you give it back.
THE WITNESS: Sure.
MR. STOFFERAHN: You don't have to say anything until he asks you a question. Could we have that marked, please.
MR. ROSENBLOOM: If you will allow me.

23

I know you're his attorney, but this is my deposition, so I will request that this will be marked, okay?
MR. STOFFERAHN: Fine.
MR. ROSENBLOOM: Thank you.
MR. STOFFERAHN: Mr. Rosenbloom, you

request that that document be marked.

MR. ROSENBLOOM: Thank you very much. Can I request that this be marked as an exhibit, please.

(Whereupon, Deposition Exhibit B was marked for identification.)

MR. ROSENBLOOM: Thank you.

BY MR. ROSENBLOOM:

Q. Can you show me, according to what has been marked as Exhibit B, which is your drawing of what you can remember of the accident, where the vehicles ended up that day?

A. Okay. We were a little before the stoplight, and there was probably — I don't remember exactly how many, but there were a few vehicles ahead of you —

Q. Uh-huh.

A. — okay, because you were behind them. Okay. And your vehicle was there, my vehicle was here. (The witness indicated.) And I bumped you, and

24

then we just pulled over to the side.

Q. Okay. And do you remember how fast you were going, any idea?

MR. STOFFERAHN: Well, I'm going to object. It's vague as to at what point.

MR. ROSENBLOOM: Okay.

MR. STOFFERAHN: You mean at impact, when he saw you?

MR. ROSENBLOOM: Well, yes, I can rephrase that for you.

BY MR. ROSENBLOOM:

Q. How fast — Two questions. How fast were you going before you saw me —

A. Okay.

Q. — any idea?

A. Yeah, not very fast. You know, I would be speculating. Not very fast.

Q. What's not very fast?

A. Twenty-five, maybe.
Q. Twenty-five?
A. Yeah, on the street, yeah.
Q. Okay. What part of your vehicle struck my vehicle?
A. My front end.
Q. Did your airbag deploy?

25

A. No, it did not.
Q. Did you have an airbag on your vehicle?
A. Yes, I do.
Q. And after the accident, you explained a little bit about what you did, you took your car to, was it an auto body?
A. Yeah. Heritage Auto Body.
Q. Okay. How were you dressed that day?
A. I believe pants, shirt.
Q. Okay. I'll accept that. Did you speak to anyone about the accident?
MR. STOFFERAHN: I'll object as to vague. At what time, Mr. Rosenbloom?
MR. ROSENBLOOM: Thank you.
BY MR. ROSENBLOOM:
Q. Anyone after the accident, immediately after the accident, did you speak to anyone?
A. No, other than when I called my wife for a ride.
Q. So — Okay. So you did speak to your wife?
A. Yes.
Q. Okay. Have you spoken with your wife anytime after the accident, on even — Well, I'll leave it at that, the question. Have you spoken to

26

your wife about the accident after the day you called her, the day of the accident?
A. Have I spoken to my wife?
Q. Have you talked about it?

A. Yes, I have spoken to my wife.
Q. Okay. You have, okay, okay. And you
may have answered this question, if you did, I
apologize for missing it, but how did you get home
that day?
A. Yeah. After I dropped off my vehicle
at Heritage Auto Body, that's when I called my wife,
and she picked me up.
Q. Okay. And what time did you arrive
home?
A. It was approximately seven o'clock.
It's — I don't remember the exact time.
Q. Did you report the accident to your
insurance agent?
A. Yes, I did.
Q. Did you take any pictures of your car?
A. I did not, no.
Q. Did anyone take pictures of your
vehicle?
A. Well, my understanding is that Heritage
Auto Body took pictures for insurance purposes.

27

Q. Okay. And I assume you got the car
fixed?
A. Yes, it is fixed.
Q. And it's drivable at this time?
A. It is drivable, yes.
Q. Okay. And it cost about $2,000, you've
already answered that; is that correct?
A. Yes, it is.
Q. And do you still have the vehicle now?
A. Yes, I do.
Q. Did you fill out or sign an accident
report?
A. No, I did not.
Q. Did you sign any accident report with
the State of Minnesota?
A. No, I did not.
Q. And so you didn't file an accident

report with the State of Minnesota, and it was $2,000
worth of damage, that's correct? There's kind of two
questions, so I can separate those, if you want.
There was $2,000 worth of damage to your vehicle?
A. That's correct.
Q. And you did not report an accident
report with the State of Minnesota?
A. With my insurance company, not with the

28

State of Minnesota, no.
Q. Okay. And do you realize that if
there's a certain amount of property damage, I believe
that you do have to — you're required to file some
report with the State?
A. No, I was not aware of that.
Q. Okay. Have you seen any of the
pleadings drafted by your lawyer regarding this case,
meaning legal documents?
A. Other than the one that was just
sitting in front of me.
Q. And that was —
MR. STOFFERAHN: The answers to
interrogatories. Plaintiff's Answers to
Interrogatories.
THE WITNESS: The answers.
MR. ROSENBLOOM: Okay.
Interrogatories, is that what we're talking about?
MR. STOFFERAHN: Plaintiff's Answers —
Defendant, Hanft's, Answers to Plaintiff's
Interrogatories.
MR. ROSENBLOOM: I would like to
introduce another exhibit. If we could mark that,
please.
(Whereupon, Deposition Exhibit C

29

was marked for identification.)
MR. ROSENBLOOM: Thank you. I've

introduced what has been marked as Exhibit B (sic), which is an Order to Dismiss, and I'll show this to your attorney.
MR. STOFFERAHN: Is that Exhibit B? I thought we were on C. Nope, that's Exhibit C.
MR. ROSENBLOOM: C. Did I say B? I am sorry, C.
MR. STOFFERAHN: Okay. Just, he hasn't asked you any questions yet. He's just showing you the document.
THE WITNESS: Okay.
MR. ROSENBLOOM: Let it — I assume counsel has no objection to this?
MR. STOFFERAHN: Objection to what? It being marked, no.
MR. ROSENBLOOM: Yeah, introduced.
MR. STOFFERAHN: I have no objection to it being marked.
BY MR. ROSENBLOOM:
Q. Okay. I'm going to ask you, Mr. Hanft, to read this. Specifically read what is marked as number 1, if you can read that, please.
A. Okay. "American Family Mutual

30

Insurance Company is hereby dismissed as a party from this action with prejudice and without cost."
Q. Okay. And you understand that document was drafted by your attorney?
MR. STOFFERAHN: Do you know whether — who drafted that document?
THE WITNESS: I — It's — I don't know who draft this document, no.
BY MR. ROSENBLOOM:
Q. Okay. Well, let's — Okay. I'll go with that. Let's say this document was drafted by any legal counsel. Do you have any understanding what the term —
A. "Release"?
Q. — "with prejudice" would mean?

MR. STOFFERAHN: I'm going to, just for the record, I'll note a continuing objection, calling for a legal conclusion, not reasonably calculated to lead to admissible evidence, but since I'm so curious, I'll let him answer the question anyhow.

MR. ROSENBLOOM: I'll withdraw the question.

BY MR. ROSENBLOOM:

Q. I would like to offer you at least another opportunity to explain why your testimony here

31

today under oath was that since the accident, you did not have any citations, you did not have any moving violations, and it appears that from the document by the Department of Public Safety, that you have said it's true that there is an illegal or improper use of lane? I'm going to ask you to explain what appears to be — or what is a — well, explain that.

A. I was — I recalled to the best of my ability. I did not recall that, and I should have.

Q. So it's your testimony under oath that to the best of your ability, you could not record — remember that? And I think the record will show that I asked you two or three times this question over and over again before you answered, purposely, so that you could — to help you remember, and you're telling me that a moving violation just a few months after the accident, it's your testimony here today that you just forgot about that?

MR. STOFFERAHN: Objection, asked and answered. He already answered that question. He said yes, he forgot about it.

MR. ROSENBLOOM: I have no further questions. This deposition is over.

THE WITNESS: Okay.

MR. STOFFERAHN: All right.

32

MR. ROSENBLOOM: Thank you.

MR. STOFFERAHN: We'll reserve the reading and signing. And we would like a copy, both regular and condensed. Thank you.

THE COURT REPORTER: Are you going to order a copy of the transcript?

MR. ROSENBLOOM: Yeah, four pages on one, that's fine.

(Whereupon, the deposition of RICHARD LEO HANFT was concluded 12:15 p.m.)

33

I, RICHARD LEO HANFT, do hereby certify that I have read the foregoing deposition and found the same to be true and correct except as follows (noting the page and line number of the change or addition as desired and the reason why):

____

RICHARD LEO HANFT

34

STATE OF MINNESOTA :

: CERTIFICATE

COUNTY OF WINONA :

BE IT KNOWN, that I, Kelly E. Kohls, Court Reporter, took the foregoing deposition of RICHARD LEO HANFT;

That the witness, before testifying, was by me first duly sworn to testify the whole truth and nothing but the truth relative to said cause;

That the testimony of said witness was recorded in shorthand by me and was reduced to typewriting under my direction;

That the foregoing deposition is a true record of the testimony given by said witness;

That the foregoing deposition, when transcribed,

was submitted for review; That I am not related to any of the parties hereto, nor an employee of them, nor interested in the outcome of the action; That the cost of the original has been charged to the party who noticed the deposition, and that all parties who ordered copies have been charged at the same rate for such copies; WITNESS MY HAND AND SEAL this 13th day of May, 2008.

____

Kelly E. Kohls, Court Reporter,
Notary Public

Lucky Rosenbloom welcomes reader responses to 612-661-0923, or email hin at l.rosenbloom@yahoo.com

Opinion 12

Blacks and Jews: what liberals don't want us to know

Teaching social studies over the years has allowed me to take notice o similarities between different cultures. To do this, one has to remove th liberal conditioning and belief that Blacks and Jews cannot come togethe because each culture has some kind of irreconcilable differences that foster hate.

We often witness this separation over and over as the liberal media woul use Malcolm X and others to demonstrate Black hate towards our Jewis brothers and sisters. If different cultures truly recognized our similaritie instead of our differences, and these similarities became the focus of ou coming together toward change, well, this would scare the living apple pi out of the liberal.

The power of cultures coming together in a social movement on loca levels would threaten the liberal hold in the urban areas. Thus, it benefi liberals to use Blacks such as Malcolm X and others to show, or attempt t show, hatred between Blacks and Jews.

Going to college learning to be an educator of political science an history, I found it easy to capture the conditioning that took place whe studying different cultures. When it came to Blacks and Jews, people desire to talk about what liberals did to help these cultures. However, when it cam to slavery and/or the Holocaust, liberal students would leave the class or shi

with observable nervousness in their seats as Jews and Blacks outlined some of the most hateful and evil acts committed on our people.

Now, I got some joy out of Blacks and Jews joining together as we joked later about the fact that we were supposed to be at odds. Because we joined together, the liberal students seemed surprised, while the conservative students seemed to accept the reality of our combined comments relevant to our historic similarities surviving hate.

In one such class, I stated something like this: "Blacks and Jews are strong people; stronger than liberal Whites, because when one looks at all we have gone through, it's by the power of God and the strength of our people we are here today." I went on to provide some similarities as other students listened with curiosity.

In a calm and loving voice liberals are used to, I advise the class that both Blacks and Jews were forcibly moved from our homelands. We have a history of slavery. To this, one student jumped in and said Whites were slaves also.

Being the Luckster that I am and staying focused, I continued by pointing out that state apparatuses and subjugation have oppressed Blacks and Jews. At this point, I noticed growing support from other Black and Jewish students. Of course, this motivated me to continue by pointing out that Blacks and Jews have been the targets of mass murders by White Christians and White civilization.

Boy! This started some classroom uneasiness! I was feeling pretty good now, so I stayed on the religion angle: Blacks and Jews have been shown in cartoons as religiously flawed, portraying Jews as Christ-killers and Blacks as worshipers of the Evil One, the devil people.

I thought my previous remarks were challenging to the class liberals, but too few seemed to be showing and/or expressing anger at that point, so I continued with a look at Black and Jewish women. Black and Jewish women, in an attempt to look cute and because our women's features have been portrayed as ugly, our women have in the past have changed hairstyles, skin tone and other features to look like White princesses.

Seeing both Jewish and Black sisters laughing in agreement, you know I had to go on. I'll admit that I was feeling pretty outstanding at this point, because Blacks and Jews in class seemed to be enjoying the change in the direction the class had taken with respect to our differences.

I looked around and said, "Show me one Black and/or Jewish person who has not experienced hate crimes, racist jokes, our churches and synagogues being burned or damaged. Show me any Black and/or Jewish person who has not been victimized in employment, housing and education, and I will show you a liberal who does not believe in raising taxes." This brought some laughter.

Being prepared for this particular day in class, I pulled out some writings from the KKK, Nazis, and those Aryan Nation types without asking consent, having students pass them around to others, which Black and Jewish students volunteered to do so. I challenged them to take a moment and read and witness for themselves what these hate-filled people say about both Blacks and Jews.

I closed by telling the class that the one thing that really bothers me is that there seem to be more liberals among both Blacks and Jews. Students knowing of my conservative beliefs quickly relaxed and laughed.

The most powerful result was that, for the remaining weeks of the class, Blacks and Jews, at one time separated, would hang together in the hallways during breaks. I told them that this is the reason liberals would rather we talk about our differences and not about our similarities.

Lucky Rosenbloom welcomes reader responses to 612-661-0923, or email him at l.rosenbloom@yahoo.com

Opinion 13

Was it liberal Democrats who egged my sign — and missed?

During the RNC, convention law enforcement personnel were on our business corner directing traffic and guiding buses and fancy cars escorted by police squads, as well as people driving by with credentials attached to their person and/or cars.

As only I could predict days before the convention while other thought I was out of my mind, having a billboard with a picture of Martin Luther King, with the sentence "Martin Luther King was Republican," gathered responses from people yelling out of passing cars in agreement or disagreement and thanking me for educating them on something they did not know.

The last day of the convention, while I was out and about, my paging system kept going off incessantly. I checked it and got a message saying, "You're a dead ni**er." Being the bright person that I am and knowing the pager number was on the King sign, I proceeded to my store at I-94 and Dale.

Upon arriving, I saw eggs on my building; the lousy people lacked dexterity throwing from their car, I postulate, and hit the building instead of the sign.

Lucky's humorous response: "I am going to post a larger sign, clean the eggs off our family business, and park myself outside (as always) with two guns on my person instead of one."

Franken v. Obama in yard sign battles

Will one of you Democrats explain this to me? I ride around the cities on my motorcycle and see a lot of Franken signs in the yards and businesses of White liberals. However, in the same yards and businesses, I don't see many Obama signs next to the Franken signs.

It appears that we are seeing the true colors of Democrats jumping ship and voting for McCain. Let me say what I have been saying for years: Blacks are great in the party of Democrats as long as you remain dependant and in your place. Obama repeats the conservative theme of self-reliance and individuation.

Could this be the reason for those lacking yard signs, or is it because liberal Democrats' real colors are showing by not supporting a Black man? You decide 2008.

Unemployment rates at all-time high?

It's being reported that unemployment is higher than ever before throughout America. I'll enter the controversy by providing you with this sagacity of insight: Do you think that unemployment is higher in the blue states and lower in the red states where we have Republican governors and Republicans in control of local politics?

The larger number of unemployed is living in states with Democrats as governors.

Governor Pawlenty's three "E"s

The Black Conservatives of Minnesota, and its chair, Lucky Rosenbloom, have learned that our governor will have what are to become the three "E" initiatives focusing on energy, education and economics.

Blacks in Minnesota must be educationally and economically prepared to compete with Whites in Minnesota within the next ten years. We must make a major shift in changing old ideas that have not worked to benefit Blacks in these two key areas. Simply put, old leadership sharing the same blame with old, failed ideas must leave the table, allowing people with fresh ideas to work with policymakers and others toward education and economic growth.

The Council on Black Minnesotans and the Urban League likely has no idea of the three "E" planning or how to provide input to the governor before the December deadline to do so. The Black Conservative does, and shall provide innovative comments around the three "E"s.

Rosenbloom urges the COBM, and others to visit the Department of Revenue website (I just told you all what to do) and submit your concerns and comments regarding ideas for energy, education, and economic growth before the December deadline.

Obama's VP pick is very alert

Brother Biden was at a rally of some sort, speaking with oomph about Obama and their issues with the Republican Party, when he noticed a former U.S. senator in the crowd and asked him to stand several times for recognition. The person was Missouri Senator Chuck Grahm in a wheelchair, unable to stand because of some kind of medical condition.

Lucky Rosenbloom welcomes reader responses to 612-661-0923, or email him at l.rosenbloom@yahoo.com

Opinion 14

Obama a challenge to low-achieving Black organizations

This month in my column, I push you to think about the meaning of Obama's recent victory. Obama means accepting no excuses for substandard performance, low expectations, and repeated poor audit findings of organizations such as the Council on Black Minnesotans (CBM).

Black organizations must step up to the calling of high expectations, bringing Blacks to a higher level of economic and educational competitiveness. If not, these organizations must be unfunded and shut down.

The past and recent audits of the CBM offer only embarrassment to the New Black American, the Obama Black American of high performance, high expectations, high quality and integrity, all of which equals Black self-esteem. This model cannot be established under the proven poor leadership at the CBM.

The CBM's staff did not consistently review a key payroll report. In addition, staff did not review another key payroll report and did not control that had backup authorization to approve hours worked and leave taken.

The council did not conduct performance reviews of the executive director, as required by statute. The council incurred expenses without adequate documentation to justify the public purpose of the expenses.

The auditors asked some questions that assisted in their findings. The question heading into the audit: For the items tested, did the council comply with significant finance-related legal requirements over its financial activities, including state laws, regulations, contracts, and applicable policies and procedures? Did the council resolve prior audit recommendations pertaining to payroll, grants, and other administrative expenditures?

The auditors concluded: The CBM did not have adequate internal controls over its payroll process to ensure that it paid employees accurately, recorded payroll transactions properly, and complied with certain payroll policies and procedures.

Don't get upset with this columnist — I am only bringing you the message of Obama's expectations of excellence in performance, without excuses. The CBM represents Black Minnesotans. Is this how we want to be viewed as new Blacks under a Black president that is an icon of Black excellence?

Let me give you some "did not's" from the audit report

The CBM's staff did not consistently review the payroll register to ensure the accuracy of payroll and personnel transactions processed in the state's payroll system. This indicated that administration did not monitor whether the council reviewed and approved the payroll registers.

The council did not review or resolve exceptions noted on the Self Service Time Entry Audit Report. The council did not control who backup authorization to approve hours had worked and leave taken in the online payroll system. The council did not conduct performance reviews of the executive director, as required by statute.

The council incurred expenses without adequate documentation to justify the public purpose of the expenses. The council was unable to substantiate the public purpose for the council's use of rental vehicles, coffee expenditures, and meals and refreshments in certain cases.

Without this documentation, some of these expenses appeared unnecessary and unreasonable. My readers, ask yourselves, with respect to the CBM's previous audits, including this recent audit, why is the issue always around money? Where is the money?

I find the following an embarrassment to Black people: Rental Cars — in fiscal year 2008, the council paid $2,632 for car rentals. In some cases, the expenses seemed unreasonable. Four of 15 rental periods extended five days or more, even though the related events were for a shorter duration.

Seven of 15 rentals recorded mileage that did not appear reasonable based on the location of the events attended by the executive director. For example, the council drove one rental car 732 miles over a seven-day period, but the council events were located in Minneapolis and surrounding areas.

Coffee — during fiscal years 2006 through 2008, the council paid $2,843 ($473 in fiscal year 2006, $1,800 in fiscal year 2007, and $570 in fiscal year 2008) to a vendor for daily coffee services provided at the council's office. The executive director explained that the council provided coffee daily because it often holds community events at the council office. The overall expenses were unreasonable.

I am going to ask you to visit www.auditor.leg.state.mn.us/fad/fadsubj.

htm#minority and read all of the CBM's audit reports. You will see a suspicious theme around money, payroll, and poor performance. With Obama as president, don't we deserve better?

The CBM needs new in-house leadership, and this columnist is not afraid to say so. What about the other CBM directors?

Lucky Rosenbloom welcomes reader responses to 612-661-0923, or email him at l.rosenbloom@yahoo.com

Opinion 15

Rochester Minnesota hate crime calls for CBM involvement

Adam Brandrup and Joshua Lee are each charged with second-degree unintentional murder in the death of 42-year-old Muhidin Mumin, who was found beaten to death in a downtown Rochester, Minnesota, alley October 1.

Olmsted County Attorney Mark Ostrem says the bias determination won't result in any changes to the murder charges filed against the two White 25-year-old Rochester men. But police are required to report bias crimes to the state.

The victim's family and Somalis in Rochester have contended from the start that it was a hate crime. This is the eighth offense this year that Rochester police have reported to the state as a bias crime. Six of them involved racial bias.

As chair of the Council on Black Minnesotans (CBM) Government Liaison Committee, I and fellow board member Charity McCoy wasted no time after hearing about this horrific incident and traveled to Rochester. We met with Deputy Prosecutor Jim Martinson, members of the Crime Victims Unit, a Somali advocate, and a family member of the victim.

Below is a summary of our visit that we provided to the Office of the Governor.

To Governor Pawlenty:

Recently, I emailed [CBM] board members about a planned trip to Rochester regarding hate crimes and the murder of a Somali man at the hands of two Whites that has been classified as a hate crime by Rochester's Police Department. No other board member except Ms. McCoy offered to go to Rochester with me; no others responded.

Upon my gathering of information, I learned from a House member and Somali advocate that the CBM has not been involved and has had no presence during the events of hate crimes in Rochester. In fact, I was advised that no one has seen anyone from the CBM in Rochester, despite the problems, since 1995. I offered an apology for this blunder.

Talking with my committee advisors, I had developed goals and objectives for my initial trip to Rochester learning of the poor communication and distrust the victim's family and others held for the County Attorney's Office and other government entities surrounding the charge of Unintentional Murder of the Somali citizen. We met with a Somalia advocate, the Deputy County Attorney, talked with members of the Crime Victims Unit, and gathered information regarding three years of reported hate crimes in the area.

We educated the Somali advocate and family member of the victim on how to use the tracking system to track the case filings and motions. We established an improved communication between family members and the Somali advocate and the entities named and outlined expectations between all entities, the Somalia advocate and attending family member. All agree to support each other and work with better communication.

We agreed to follow the trial to its conclusion and offer assistance as needed. All involved appreciated our involvement and encouraged our continued involvement as needed.

This will continue to be a delicate operation as the trial gets underway, holding and fostering clear communication and trust. Therefore, it is important that board members do not do anything to disrupt our accomplishments in such a short period which would undermine our efforts.

We were advised of concerns in Rochester's schools, also. However, an agreement was reached to focus on these issues after the trial. We had a productive meeting clearing up rumors and empowering those we met with, leading to a more positive view of the CBM.

We established expectations with the crime victim's office with respect to benefits the victim's family is entitled to under law. We educated the Somali advocate on using the Register of Actions, allowing him to track the case of the two suspects, thus empowering the advocate to be aware of motions and being in court during such motions with our expectations that family will be accompanied by a member of the crime victim's office.

We gathered information on three years of reported hate crimes in Rochester. With all of this, we acted with high standards, leading to the immediate, concise and competent actions expressed in our summary.

The plan is to return and train our brothers in establishing Focus Groups with a mission, goals, objectives and strategy to deal with racial tensions in Rochester. We promised to monitor the trial of the men charged with the murder; therefore, we shall.

We created a tone which the CBM can follow up on in one visit to Rochester, getting things done without delay. Therefore, my further involvement will be as an opinion news columnist monitoring and holding government accountable to the Somali community.

Our appreciation to Ms. McCoy for her concern and stepping up to Obama's high expectations of Blacks working in organizations such as the CBM.

Lucky Rosenbloom welcomes reader responses to 612-661-0923, or email him at l.rosenbloom@yahoo.com

Opinion 16

Black youth have a chance in Ramsey County-State of Minnesota

Ramsey County Juvenile Detention Center owns some impressive statistics showing their efforts to keep low-level offenders out of the judicial system. Once in the justice system, it's hard to extricate yourself from that system even as a juvenile. Thus, low-level offenders run the risk of becoming more serious offenders if the answer is always lockup.

A lot of people worked hard to develop Ramsey County's Juvenile Detention Alternatives efforts to keep low-level offenders in contact with their families and communities by releasing youth to parents or meaningful placements in our community instead of locking them up.

The following are impressive results of the project with respect to juvenile bookings and changes over the years:

Ramsey County Juvenile Detention Center Admissions for the years 2006, 2007 and 2008: admissions for detention 3,193 to 2,575 to 1,913, a 40 percent decrease; admissions for new offense 1,654 to 1,344 to 874, a 47 percent decrease; admissions for probation violation 584 to 418 to 268, a 45 percent decrease; admissions for warrant 589 to 530 to 476, a 19 percent decrease.

I asked Steve Poynter, superintendent of Ramsey County Juvenile Corrections, to respond:

"I have had the privilege of being the superintendent of the Ramsey County Juvenile Detention Center (JDC) since 2001. Since our involvement with the Juvenile Detention Alternatives Initiative (JDAI) began approximately three years ago, I have witnessed and been able to be part of something that I believe will positively impact the community, the juvenile justice system, and most importantly the youth of Ramsey County for years to come.

"The outcomes of this initiative have resulted in an objective screening tool to determine who should be admitted to JDC, collaboration amongst the community and the numerous agencies in the juvenile justice system, and improved the conditions of confinement in the JDC to name a few."

A well known organizer is one of many who have played a strong role in making the JDAI a big reality in reaching out to our youth. Knowing that locking up low-level offenders is not always the answer, Chris Crutchfield, deputy director for community relations, responds:

"The Ramsey County Juvenile Detention Alternatives Initiative (JDAI) is implementing reforms to reduce the number of juveniles placed in secure detention and to eliminate racial disparities in the juvenile justice system.

"Community members and public officials are working together on this effort to achieve better long-term results for kids. The initiative seeks to create more effective, community-based alternatives to juvenile detention for youth who do not pose a significant risk to public safety.

"(The focus is on the detention that occurs when a juvenile is awaiting court hearings, not the confinement ordered after a youth is found guilty of committing a delinquent act.)

"Launched in 2006, this partnership is part of a national movement driven by research showing that, controlling for all other factors, children placed in secure detention tends to have more problems in the long term than those who aren't put in detention, in terms of school performance, criminal involvement, and mental and physical health."

"Nobody is saying that youths who commit crimes should not be held accountable," says St. Paul Police Chief John Harrington. "What we're saying is that unnecessary detention can do more harm than good — at great expense to taxpayers and public safety."

I want to offer my appreciation to all of the players that made the JDAI a meaningful, authentic, and right and proper tool to be used towards giving our youth a chance at change, the change Obama preaches about — the chance to change and be productive young men and women in our neighborhoods.

Launa Newman's spirit lives on

The passing of a wonderful woman in Minnesota

Love, joy and peace of God surround the spirit of a wonderful, undaunted, and remarkable woman we have come to know and remember as Ms. Launa Newman. Launa Newman's spirit lives on in every future issue of the *Minnesota Spokesman-Recorder*, her family and second family being all the people over the years that have made reading the *MSR* a part of our weekly lives.

Let us share in the love, joy and peace that surround Ms. Launa Newman's spirit, knowing that we shall have a glorious reunion in Heaven, whereby we shall meet again. Until that time, find relief in her work and the smile in the many pictures we have seen of her since she joined a team of God's most precious Angels.

Lucky Rosenbloom welcomes reader responses to 612-661-0923, or email him at l.rosenbloom@yahoo.com

Opinion 17

Blacks and Jews: what liberals don't want us to know?

Teaching social studies over the years has allowed me to take notice of similarities between different cultures. To do this, one has to remove the liberal conditioning and belief that Blacks and Jews cannot come together because each culture has some kind of irreconcilable differences that fosters hate.

We often witness this separation over and over as the liberal media would use Malcolm X and others to demonstrate Black hate towards our Jewish brothers and sisters. If different cultures truly recognized our similarities instead of our differences, and these similarities became the focus of our coming together toward change, well, this would scare the living apple pie out of the liberal.

The power of cultures coming together in a social movement on local levels would threaten the liberal hold in the urban areas. Thus, it benefits liberals to use Blacks such as Malcolm X and others to show, or attempt to show, hatred between Blacks and Jews.

Going to college learning to be an educator of political science and history, I found it easy to capture the conditioning that took place when studying different cultures. When it came to Blacks and Jews, people desired to talk about what liberals did to help these cultures. However, when it came to slavery and/or the Holocaust, liberal students would leave the class or shift with observable nervousness in their seats as Jews and Blacks outlined some of the most hateful and evil acts committed on our people.

Now, I got some joy out of Blacks and Jews joining together as we joked later about the fact that we were supposed to be at odds. Because we joined together, the liberal students seemed surprised, while the conservative students seemed to accept the reality of our combined comments relevant to our historic similarities surviving hate.

In one such class, I stated something like this: "Blacks and Jews are strong people; stronger than liberal Whites, because when one looks at all we have gone through, it's by the power of God and the strength of our people we are here today." I went on to provide some similarities as other students listened with curiosity.

In a calm and loving voice liberals are used to, I advise the class that both Blacks and Jews were forcibly moved from our homelands. We have a history of slavery. To this, one student jumped in and said Whites were slaves also.

Being the Luckster that I am and staying focused, I continued by pointing out that state apparatuses and subjugation have oppressed Blacks and Jews. At this point, I noticed growing support from other Black and Jewish students. Of course, this motivated me to continue by pointing out that Blacks and Jews have been the targets of mass murders by White Christians and White civilization.

Boy! This started some classroom uneasiness! I was feeling pretty good now, so I stayed on the religion angle: Blacks and Jews have been shown in cartoons as religiously flawed, portraying Jews as Christ-killers and Blacks as worshipers of the Evil One, the devil people.

I thought my previous remarks were challenging to the class liberals, but too few seemed to be showing and/or expressing anger at that point, so I continued with a look at Black and Jewish women. Black and Jewish women, in an attempt to look cute and because our women's features have been portrayed as ugly, our women have in the past have changed hairstyles, skin tone and other features to look like White princesses.

Seeing both Jewish and Black sisters laughing in agreement, you know I had to go on. I'll admit that I was feeling pretty outstanding at this point, because Blacks and Jews in class seemed to be enjoying the change in the direction the class had taken with respect to our differences.

I looked around and said, "Show me one Black and/or Jewish person who has not experienced hate crimes, racist jokes, our churches and synagogues being burned or damaged. Show me any Black and/or Jewish person who has not been victimized in employment, housing and education, and I will show you a liberal who does not believe in raising taxes." This brought some laughter.

Being prepared for this particular day in class, I pulled out some writings from the KKK, Nazis, and those Aryan Nation types without asking consent, having students pass them around to others, which Black and Jewish students volunteered to do so. I challenged them to take a moment and read and witness for themselves what these hate-filled people say about both Blacks and Jews.

I closed by telling the class that the one thing that really bothers me is that there seem to be more liberals among both Blacks and Jews. Students knowing of my conservative beliefs quickly relaxed and laughed.

The most powerful result was that, for the remaining weeks of the class,

Blacks and Jews, at one time separated, would hang together in the hallways during breaks. I told them that this is the reason liberals would rather we talk about our differences and not about our similarities.

Lucky Rosenbloom welcomes reader responses to 612-661-0923, or email him at l.rosenbloom@yahoo.com

Opinion 18

We must drop the victim role to prosper

We must ask ourselves the question, "Why is it that other people from different cultures have achieved substantial economic gains, higher education levels, higher home and business ownership, and more, as compared to African Americans?"

There are three reasons: (1) The federal, state, and local liberal politicians who control our community; (2) Black community leaders who make excuse after excuse for their blunders, and who by doing so have excused our people into becoming victims of blame and doom; and (3) we have failed to give up the acceptance of victimization that is so intensely highly wrought in our culture.

Now, the victim position has failed because we have no real negotiation based within the liberal structure. We are duped into believing that White blame will manifest into business opportunities. The liberals have not and will not let go of White dispensation in our communities. Black leadership must realize that the concept of guilt premeditated at White liberals has a deceptive perception of power, and they (White liberals) have used this guilt game as a way to oppress us economically.

Other cultures not experienced in the guilt game gather themselves collectively to create business and economic opportunity. This independence allows these cultures to thrive. Our leaders have led us into doom while excusing this direction as our being victims.

The new liberal electronic form of discrimination

Young Blacks and one sister in particular, have reported to me that most corporations are now accepting job applications via e-mail/internet. The information goes through a database. The database selects key words for the selected position.

Anyone who makes it through this process is sent an electronic application and could be discriminated against based on one's cultural name, ethnicity, or community. Thus, living over North or in South Minneapolis, or in other areas where negative projections are seen in the liberal media, one could easily be rejected. If you make it to an interview, the job description suddenly changes outside of the required qualifications of your background that initially got you the interview.

One sister believes that she receives calls from potential employers after going through the electronic process, and if a voice message is left on an answering machine with her standard voice mail greeting, a message is left confirming a time for an interview. Once the sister calls back to confirm, this is when liberal discrimination begins. Oh! The name Jill Scottishberg sounds like a Black person.

I want to thank the sister who sent me this response. These are the new and perhaps most hidden and protected forms of liberal discrimination into the next century, and Black civil rights organizations don't know how to deal with this sophisticated racism because it is camouflaged using electronic technology.

President Clinton educated the liberal racist

The cool brother Clinton, the "first Black president," in his 1997 inaugural speech asked over one million college folks to read to America's children. Slick Clinton was using a well-known Democrat paradigm of redemptive liberalism to create White power by establishing the Black reading problem as a stipulation that implied that the White liberal teacher is hope for the poor student. This was a slick way of fostering the myth of affirmative action, which is often seen as a way to help the marginal Black.

Mayor Rybak responds to White liberal deaths

Since the Iraq War began, we have had 30 Minnesotans killed serving our country. Since 2001, we have had 224 homicides in Minneapolis. Two were White and killed in business areas at the hands of criminals of color.

Where are the Black leaders to challenge Rybak, to have discourse about his loud action for more police and resources when people of color are killing people of color? The liberal mayor has demonstrated redemptive racism, yet no Black leader made a serious issue of this inept action. Why? Because they are wearing min-skirts and hot pants and are afraid to speak out for fear of losing any crumbs given in the past to keep the Black warriors from becoming conservative.

In 2004, the violent crime rate for Minneapolis was more than two and a half times the national average. The murder rate for the nation was 5.5 per 100, 0000. The Luckster does not claim to be an expert, or even good in math, but this means that the Minneapolis rate was almost three times the national average, 14.1 per 100,000.

The FBI statistics indicate an increase in crime in Murderapo— I mean, Minneapolis. Crime across the nation decreased while crime here increased. Mayor Rybak, where were you before the 2006 uptown and Block E killings? All of these crimes occur under the liberal DFL-controlled community.

Lucky Rosenbloom welcomes reader responses to 612-661-0923, or email him at l.rosenbloom@yahoo.com

Opinion 19

Why Blacks avoid studying philosophy

When I was growing up, philosophy seemed to me a discipline for Whites who hated Blacks and were for the privileged. I often thought of philosophy having a sign under the discipline reading "For Whites Only."

Then I discovered a Black philosopher and university educator named Charles W. Mills and read his book *Blackness Visible: Essays on Philosophy and Race* (1998). I am going to offer some of his ideas followed by my comments. I hope you find this very inspirational.

Mills promotes the idea that philosophy as a discipline has done an injustice to Blacks in that it has perpetuated the subjugation, slavery and domination of Blacks by White society by refusing to recognize and address social injustices. He refers to "the self-sustaining dynamics of the "Whiteness' of philosophy…, the conceptual or theoretical Whiteness of the discipline. This alone would be sufficient to discourage Black graduate students contemplating a career in the academy."

Mills is pushing us to ask ourselves what it is about this discipline's practitioners and about society that allows it to remain appealing to Whites and not Blacks. Is this the one thing American Whites are trying to hold onto? Heck, Blacks are into golf, hockey and tennis. What's left, America?

"But the responses of Blacks pose more of a challenge," says Mills, "because for the most part Blacks are simply not mentioned in classic philosophy text." We see the theme of the author building with force to show that Blacks have been meaningless within the discipline of philosophy.

"But in Western philosophy there is no rationale for Black subordination in particular (as against arguments for slavery in general)." The author suggests that philosophy assists in the subjugation and the acceptance of inferiority of the races because the discipline seems to have accepted these constructs for lack of challenge.

"No protests against the traditional theory of slavery emerged from the great seventeenth-centuries authorities on law, or from such philosophers and men-of-letters as Descartes." We have to interpret Mills' comment here as saying that, because of Descartes' failure to attack the evils of slavery, this can only means that philosophers supported this evilness.

Perhaps, if the great philosophers of that era had challenged slavery as being wrong and stood against the evil as did others, this stance would have given philosophy a more favorable view within the Black culture. Instead, philosophy has become somewhat adversarial within Black culture, some kind of taboo, like staying away from the Ku Klux Klan.

Regarding the system based on Negro slave labor, Mills says, "For a time, most jurists and philosophers met this discrepancy simply by ignoring it." How can Blacks respect or be interested in a discipline that fostered slavery? In the Black community we have a saying: "To ignore evil is to support evil."

No wonder Metro State reportedly searched the world but could not find anyone Black to teach philosophy. Anyone Black, such as Mills, preaching the truth as he does about this discipline, is surely isolated within this discipline for bringing out its dark side.

"A lot of philosophy is White guys jerking off," says Mills. I'll leave this one to your interpretation.

"African American philosophy is thus inherently, definitional oppositional, the philosophy produced by property that does not remain silent but insists on speaking and contesting status." Here the author is saying that Blacks and philosophy are in natural conflict, a conflict rooted in hatred towards Blacks, because of the discipline's failure to challenge evils such as slavery.

"Western philosophy abstracts away from what has been the central feature of the lives of Africans transported against their will to the Americas: the denial of Black humanity and the reactive, defiant assertion of it."

I am not accepting that Mills has a strong dislike for philosophy. Mills loves philosophy and is saddened that the discipline failed to be a voice to challenge the injustices of slavery.

Where was the discipline of philosophy during the Civil Rights Movement? The discipline Mills loves so well lacks what so many other disciplines are recognized for — the fight for equality. Mills feels as though philosophy has forever lost its place in the struggle for justice and equality in American history.

In conclusion, based on the statements provided by Mills and my comments, I believe the author wants the reader to believe that philosophy has assisted in the oppression and subjugation of Blacks in America because of its failure to challenge social injustices. This alone goes far in explaining the discipline's inability to attract African American students.

Lucky Rosenbloom welcomes reader responses to 612-661-0923, or email him at l.rosenbloom@yahoo.com

Opinion 20

Coming to a liberal city near you:
the New Black American Political Machine

Democrats' liberal policies keep people dependent using social policies so heavy to lift during your bench press that these liberal policies create and hold you down in poverty. The heavy weights of welfare make it difficult for Black liberals to lift themselves into capitalism because of too much governmental regulation designed to prevent Blacks from starting businesses, which establish self-reliance and responsibility for our families.

Liberal policies such as welfare and other handouts keep Blacks weighted down in water, never to surface, while suffering the spiritual death of waiting, begging, and keeping hope alive in a liberal system of high taxes. Liberals working their way out of this liberal bondage of dependency into self-reliance are forced to pay high taxes supporting welfare and other handout programs, limiting the food on your tables and taxing you out of your homes and other ownership investments.

Those of you reading my column know much of what is said is the truth. How many of you, after obtaining higher education and landing that good job, at one time were accepting of liberal polices but now is upset because of the money coming out of your checks to support welfare and other liberal policies?

Come on — many of you can now be heard saying those favorite words, "I am tired of all this money coming out of my check for people on welfare." Remember, you could at one time have been one of those people. An education, a job, home ownership, having a business and paying high taxes year after year makes one a conservative real fast.

What really scares a liberal is when one sees a Black parent heavily involved in their child's education, because the liberal must see him/herself as the great White teaching hope. Liberals do not like seeing Black parents involved in their schools, because this means more control those parents have over curriculum, the teacher unions, accountability and measured outcomes.

You can see the panic if each one of you told 10 other Black parents, and they told 10 other Black parents, that on the first and last Tuesday of each month we are all going to spend two hours in any given school. Wow!

Black parents in schools just two days each month would drive liberal teachers crazy who are doing nothing but collecting a paycheck. Organize in your child's school, and make this happen now.

We should have a major movement in our community advising young people to prepare for the jobs of the 21st century. If a Black teen put as much time into his/her books, reading, math and social studies as they do smoking weed, playing basketball, hanging out on the street looking cool and waiting to be MVP of his home play station, our community would turn out wondrous scholars.

Out of high school, I joined the military. With the discipline I already had on entering, matched with the drive and never-give-up attitude learned from the military and my parents, I was prepared to improvise, overcome and adapt to working and pursuing education, meeting the mandate of any given societal change.

Having the mindset of a dependent liberal would have destroyed my entire character, and we witness this destruction of our youth today. They are not victims of being ghettoized, but rather of being liberalized into failure.

Liberal policies have caused destruction in the Black family system. From the acceptance of gay marriage to moving prayer out of schools, these policies have all taken away from the traditional Black family and God as our endurance. We see HIV, gays, all embarrassments to the Black family, and all because of liberal policies that Black preachers will not denounce in their pulpits because of being more committed to the Democrats than the word of God.

Black liberals have allowed our people to enter into a steady course of Willie Lynch self-destruction by accepting the liberal message that gay is fine, anti-God and anti-Black values being God, family and moral values. We must repent, turn away from this evilness, and reclaim our family values.

The New Black American Political Machine must give up the liberal policies of self-destruction and work for lower taxes, calling for liberals not to penalize earnings and investments; calling on government to create a transparent and accountable budget; privatizing public services; capping taxes and expenditures; funding our students and not failing neighborhood schools; reforming Medicaid programs; reforming Welfare; and protecting employees from the politics of unions and racism.

This is the New Black Movement. Organize and start this movement in your areas today. Make it happen. The shorties will be glad you did.

Minneapolis Civil Rights Commission

Why are so many liberals afraid of Michael Jordan and Ron Brandon? Ninety-nine percent of the perpetrators of racism and discrimination in the city of Minneapolis are Democrats. If I were such a Democrat, I wouldn't want our two unafraid brothers around.

Onward!

Lucky Rosenbloom welcomes reader responses to 612-661-0923, or email him at l.rosenbloom@yahoo.com

Reader responses email mnbrc@hotmail.com.

Opinion 21

Liberal policies very dangerous to your health

I'm not ignoring anything.

I exercise, run about 15 miles each week, lift weights, pop 80 pushups in one minute, and work to build muscular strength and muscular endurance. So, I'm not ignoring anything.

This Black Conservative will not ignore chest pains. No, not the Luckster. If I ever have chest pain that feels like 30 liberals sat on my chest, you best believe that the Luckster is going to save money and hold down future costs by going to the closest emergency room.

Hearing liberals beg all the time can cause a conservative like me pain in my left arm, and after many attempts to talk sense into a liberal with added pain in my jaw, matched with sweating and shortness of breath, well, you can be assured the Luckster is headed to the emergency room. This is a sign that liberal policies are giving me a heart attack.

This Black Conservative is not ignoring shortness of breath. Man, I listened to a recent Democrat presidential debate. None of those clowns answered questions with substance. The irony of it all could cause anyone to have walked at least one block, or to have run downstairs for some juice and back up the stairs to continue listening.

If I experience shortness of breath after this kind of movement, motivated by liberals whose only real answer to any question about programs is taking money out of our pockets to support absurd ideas, the Luckster is not going to ignore this. I'm going to see a conservative doctor.

Watching Hillary Clinton talk about ending the war in Iraq, yet voting to fund the war, makes me want to choke. Listening to Hillary Clinton makes me so sick, I, don't want to eat. However, if my pants no longer fit thanks to junk food, the Luckster is going to a conservative doctor, because listening to Hillary may have caused me to develop cancer.

A lot of what liberals say is a bunch of crap (I substituted crap for the desired word). It would be nice if we could just eat up liberal policies for digesting and flushing. However, their policies are worse than any food poisoning.

So, if their policies digest with blood in my urine, or stool, you got it —

I'm going to see a conservative doctor. You must understand that it's not my desire to look at digested liberal waste, but it's integral to my health to do exactly that from time to time after eating liberal policies.

Let me stick with this urination of liberal policies. Let's say that liberal policies have been so damaging to Black people that I had to put their policies in a blender with a bottle of Gatorade and drink their policies in order to prevent further harm to Black people. Taking this risk because of my care for you, the reader, well, let's say that this would cause changes in my urination pattern.

I am getting up too many times at night to pi## liberal policies. I have accomplished my goal of weakening liberal policies, but now my urination looks weak also, and it's difficult to get my urination started. See, it's possible that liberal policies have given the Luckster prostate cancer.

I will not ignore these symptoms. Say it with me: I'm going to see a conservative doctor.

This has to work. It's time to get the Minnesota Democrat platform. Once in my possession, I'll kick it all up and down the halls of the local DFL, the halls of the city council that is doing nothing about the newly created jobs with respect to the bridge collapse.

Why are Blacks fighting for these jobs? Don't blame this on Pawlenty.

If the Luckster has any leg swelling or accumulation of fluid in my ankles or feet, that means kicking these policies may have caused heart, kidney or liver disease. Say it with me once again: I'm going to see a conservative doctor.

Liberal policies make my skin itch. Sometimes, reading liberal policies, hearing liberals speak, and hearing liberal doomsday preachers cause skin lesions. If these liberal policy lesions fail to heal after a few days — get this — those liberal policies and speakers have ruined my circulation and given me diabetes or skin cancer.

If those liberal policy wounds become larger or change color and shape, say it with me one last time: I'm going to see a conservative doctor.

There is a message here for Black men. We like to stay away from physicians until it's too late. Don't ignore warning signs that liberal policies have affected your health. As soon as you experience any of the signs expressed herein, go and see a conservative doctor, because liberal prescriptions will not work. However, this could be a good malpractice suit.

Women, there is a message in this column for you also.

Lucky Rosenbloom welcomes reader responses to 612-661-0923, or email him at l.rosenbloom@yahoo.com

Opinion 22

Anyone desire to challenge my opinion?

I find four concepts that keep Blacks from becoming economically and educationally competitive.

1. Double standards
2. Preferential treatment
3. Provisions for cultural differences
4. Entitlements

As I write in my book (Liberal Racism Creates the Black Conservative) the reason other minorities, including people from Africa, arrive to this great place (America) and augment their lives are because they have not accepted these concepts.

I attended a meeting on October 14, 2008, at the Martin Luther King Center, the subject being economics. I heard people blaming Republicans, Pawlenty, banks, I could continue for Black failure among others areas private business.

If my dad (Tiger Jack) begged banks, government, or accepted one of the Liberal concepts of doom (see 1-4 above) his tiny store would not have been moved to the Historical Society, the street would have not been named after him, well, if he had waited on, begged anyone, he would not be the example of Black hard work without excuses that many have read about, seen news reports about, or visit the Historical Society to learn about.

How can anyone Black organization preach and/or accept this begging acceptance, and preach the same doom day's theories that have failed our community for years?

I make $900 in five-hours (more than some make in a week) plus, income from drafting pleadings for lawyers, music from my musical talent, my book, two-jobs and other talents. If I had begged government to help me instead of working overtime, several jobs to save money and start my business, I would not be sharing this with you now. If I had waited for handouts, blamed the White man for holding me back, instead of working harder than the other guy, I would not have degrees and education in Paralegal, Education, Law Enforcement and Social Sciences.

Blacks have to let go of those agencies that teach us failure by always depending on government programs to help us start businesses, or matriculating into College, if we are to be" race competitive" in the coming century. Any agency, any organization that promotes begging, or waiting for some kind of handout, a loan that we blame the White man for not getting, is to promote Black doom with respect to Education and Economic growth. Heck, I never got a loan to start my business; I worked hard, overtime, got the money and did it on my own. Yes. Just like Tiger Jack. People that wait for the handout, place blame, wait for 1-4, are not doing anything, accept to hate on me, or accuse me of having some kind of silver-spoon.

In my book, I promote the idea that performance does not follow self-esteem. When you refuse to wait on the White man, or agencies, when you work harder than the other guy to get what you want, this allows performance. Thus, performance equals high expectations. High expectations equal self-reliance. Self-reliance equals successful Black business people.

I have attended meetings in the community for over 20 years. I listen to the same old Liberal concepts of doom and failure. When, are our leaders, the leaders of agencies, including members of the Council on Black Minnesotans going to learn to stop promoting dependency? Our social programs are left begging for money to serve members of our community. Funding, funding. If we don't get enough, we have to stop this, or that. Let's blame Pawlenty.

With all the money people say we have in the community, yet, if we truly do spend it outside of our community. You have no one to blame but yourselves.

After the meeting, I went to my families store to do a security check. A white man stopped by and said, "Are you Lucky" I answered yes. He continued "I just wanted to let you know of my appreciation for you and your family, bringing people together, taking the bold positions that you do, by the way, May I register for your next gun class and get a copy of your boo?" Now, if I had waited, begged government, banks, or waited for some other handout, that White man would had never known about my business, my book. He would have never stopped because I would not have been there. By waiting for handouts, Blacks keep themselves from not being there.

A story: I have a Black youth that wanted to start his own t-shirt business with designs. He could not get a loan, did not know where to turn for help after he had been turned away by agencies. He had accepted concepts 1-4. I told him to bring me some of his works. He did. After looking at his work, I responded "you mean to tell me with all this talent to make money; you are going to wait on someone to give you something to start? Get your butt a job, two-jobs, save enough money to buy your supplies, by your shirts, have some flyers printed" He did so. Now, he has contracts to do business with companies. At times, as he walks by my store, people stop him on the street to do business. He offers me thanks, for which I refuse to take. My thanks are seeing him walk by my store with shirts in his hands, saying "gotta keep moving, got get my orders done."

Black leaders from all agencies must teach self-reliance and get away from this group agency of blame and failure.

Read more about this in my book Liberal Racism Creates the Black Conservative.

An open letter to the Chair, Council on Black Minnesotans
Brother Collins
October 16, 2008

Brother Collins: The Council on Black Minnesotans Board of Directors had an agreement that Community Forums would not be conducted on the same nights as of Board meetings to prevent interference with Council's business. This agreement was in fact violated, which demonstrates disrespect to Board Members. The reason you provided for this serious Breach of agreement as not being aware of the agreement, which could have been reviewed in previous minutes and/or others on the Executive Committee could have advised, or any time crunch, both lack substance and does not offer reasonable explanations for such a serious breach that violates an agreement sustained by the entire Board.

This type of behavior at a public meeting does not serve the best interest of the people we are to represent. In fact, it's that this type of behavior stimulates actions such as Board Members walking out of meetings to bust of taking care of business; including behavior such as a male Board member calling a female Board Member dull and stupid in a public meeting attended by community members and elected officials.

This type of outright, ostensible disrespect must cease immediately, or this community member will take legal action or any other civil action against the Board because this type of behavior does not serve our community well, when we have this plethora of issues hurting our people daily.

In the October's Board meeting, the Chair mentioned having a meeting with Annie (a member of the governor's office) several times, however, failed to provide the full content of that meeting. Therefore, at our next Board meeting, I demand that the Board, the public is advised of the full content of that meeting because you delivered this message in a public meeting.

The Council on Black Minnesotans is the highest ranking entity representing Black people in the State of Minnesota. For those of you reading this letter, don't you feel you deserve better than members walking out of meetings, or a brother calling a sister dull and stupid because of a disagreement on any given subject matter?

This community member shall continue to hold the Council on Black Minnesotans accountable. It's not important that I win a popularity contest. It's important the Black community wins measurable accountability from organizations such as the Council on Black Minnesotans and your tax dollars are being used for more than name calling during Board meetings and folks walking out for no other reason, but to bust up business. Don't think this is true? I'll give you a free tape of that meeting.

Lucky Rosenbloom welcomes reader responses to 612-661-0923, or email him at l.rosenbloom@yahoo.com

Opinion 23

Democrats Block Black Vote in Minnesota

80% of Minnesotans favor requiring photo ID to vote. This is an overwhelming majority. The Minnesota Democrats failed to pass this legislation. The Democrats blocked the bill and the Black legislative Democrats must be held accountable for allowing this to happen. Indiana enjoyed record voter turnout after enacting a photo ID requirement to vote.

If legislators intend to defy the will of their constituents, they are at least obligated to provide evidence that people will be disenfranchised. Democrats could not provide this fact, thus, switched to using seniors as the new scapegoats to deny Black voting in the subterfuge.

Our election system is full of holes that undermine public confidence in the outcome of our elections. Most often we see this in the Black community. Requiring the use of Minnesota identification, opposed to a stupid utility bill, would have empowered the Black vote in areas outside of the urban districts.

Every eligible Black voter deserves to have the confidence that his or her vote will not be undermined by a system left wide open to potential errors and abuse.

The voter ID bill will empower and enfranchise the disaffected by providing a free ID to people who don't have one and can't afford one. It's nearly impossible to function in modern society without ID.

The double standard for unverified same-day registrations and verified advance registrations violates the concept of equal protection under the law and is socially unjust. We must ask ourselves as Black people the reason Democrats wanted nothing to do with voter identification at the voting locations throughout Minnesota?

Many improper voter registrations are rejected only after that voter's ballot has been cast and counted. It can take up to six months to verify the legitimacy of a same-day voter registration. I have seen Blacks leave the voting place because of no utility bill. How many of you carry a dog gone utility bill in your pocket? The Democrats voted against voter identification because it was introduced by Republicans. The Democrats put a serious hurt on the

Black community to simply flex their new gained power. We must as what are Champion and Hayden going to do about this wickedness from member in their own party?

After reconstruction, to the 1964 voting rights act, Blacks and women have fought hard to augment our right to vote. The Democrats diminished that right by voting down a Bill that would have empowered the Black and Women vote recently.

I have seen Blacks walk away and not return to vote because of not having a utility bill. The law enforcing ones right to vote by having proper identification would have taken away this abuse and empowered Blacks and women in urban Minnesota because this proper identification would have empowered the voter by not being turned away. How, many of you carry a utility bill daily opposed to your identification?

Testifying in front of Democrats for this bill, allowed me to feel what it must have been like for Blacks to testify and fight Democrats like Gov. George Wallace and Bull Conner that were against the Civil Rights moment and voting rights for Blacks. Wallace and Conner would have been proud of the performance of each Democrat that voted the voter I.D. bill down.

Lucky Rosenbloom is on the Board of directors on the State Council on Black Minnesotans and would like to know you're opinion on this subject at *Lucky Rosenbloom welcomes reader responses to 612-661-0923, or email him at l.rosenbloom@yahoo.com*

Opinion 24

Black man with a gun

The following is an actual transcript whereby, I defeated liberals afraid of me because of my legal right to carry a gun in the State of Minnesota. These people were co-workers at the Hubert H. Humphrey Job Corp- Center in St. Paul. The Court concluded in my favor and indicated possible harassment and credibility issues with the HHH, witnesses. I represented myself against Minnesota's top law firm and won using Black man with a gun. My brain

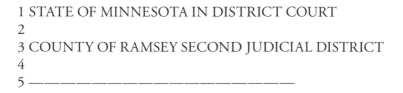

STATE OF MINNESOTA IN DISTRICT COURT

COUNTY OF RAMSEY SECOND JUDICIAL DISTRICT

————————————————————————

Chris Kuhn, O/B/O Hubert Humprey
Job Corps Center,
Petitioner,

vs. File No. C3-05-100886

Maryland Rosenbloom, EXCERPT FROM PROCEEDINGS

Respondent.

———————————————————————

The above-entitled matter came on for hearing before the Honorable Ann Leppanen, one of the Referees of the above-named Court, on February 8, 2006, at the Juvenile and Family Justice Center, St. Paul, MN.

APPEARANCES:

Huyen Le Phan, Attorney At Law, appeared with and on behalf of the Petitioners.

Maryland Rosenbloom, Respondent, appeared Pro Se.

P R O C E E D I N G S

(The Following is an excerpt from the proceedings had as follows:)

... THE COURT: I think all of you would like to be done sooner then that. Is it realistic, Mr. Rosenbloom, for you to be able to put in your testimony — and I'm not talking about cross-examination — your testimony and finish up with this witness in half an hour.

MR. ROSENBLOOM: Are we taking today?

THE COURT: Not today.

MR. ROSENBLOOM: Okay. Yes, I think that's reasonable.

THE COURT: I'm going to hold everybody to these time frames. Ms. Phan.

MS. PHAN: Yes?

THE COURT: Give me some sense as to what you

think — well, actually let me back up, because Mr. Rosenbloom raised an issue about calling a different witness. And you were talking about calling Chris Kuhn, is that correct.

MR. ROSENBLOOM: Yes.

MS. PHAN: And I'm going to object to that, Your Honor, based upon your order which clearly states that the witness lists must be exchanged between the parties on or before January 18th of 2005 — six.

MR. ROSENBLOOM: Your Honor, you have already been flexible for Counsel. And Mr. Kuhn is the author of the original temporary order.

THE COURT: Thank you, Mr. Rosenbloom, that was going to be my response. Mr. Kuhn did bring the petition on behalf of Hubert Humphrey Job Corps Center, and while I realize that he's not the only person, he certainly was the person signing the petition, and I would consider him to not have necessarily needed to be disclosed any more than Mr. Rosenbloom would need to have been disclosed.

MS. PHAN: The only thing, Your Honor, is the fact that Mr. Kuhn doesn't have any personal first-hand knowledge regarding these facts. He was asked to step in because he was the Acting Center Director upon advice from the Court as someone who should have been named. It should have been Karen Von Guten because she's the one that has first-hand personal knowledge, he was just asked to step in because he was there. And if you're —

MR. ROSENBLOOM: Your Honor —

MS. PHAN: — if the Court says he has to testify he'll come up and testify. But his knowledge regarding facts giving rise to everything are very limited. And the affidavit is focused on and completed by Karen Von Guten, not Mr. Kuhn, is that correct?

MR. KUHN: That's correct.

MR. ROSENBLOOM: Your Honor —

THE COURT: Hold on. I think Mr. Rosenbloom does have the right to call the person who's named in the caption, and it may be that Mr. Kuhn has limited information, and then that would be very quickly disposed of.

So let's assume Mr. Rosenbloom can dispose of his case in half an hour.

MR. ROSENBLOOM: Your Honor, I would like to entertain a motion for dismissal. Its Counsel's testimony for this Court that Mr. Kuhn had no knowledge really what was going on, yet he signed an affidavit to the court on an affidavit — sworn testimony, Your Honor, listing what he considered to be facts.

And now its Counsel's testimony that he was not at Job Corps, he has been gone for a while, and he really had no knowledge what was going on. So he files a complaint based on hearsay —

THE COURT: Okay. Stop.

MR. ROSENBLOOM: — and lack of relation —

THE COURT: Stop. One of the problems we have and that I may have made an assumption correctly or incorrectly, so lets clarify this point before we go much further — I have the petition.

On page two of two, there's a notarized signature, now the signature is as illegible as the notary's signature, so I just made an assumption that this was Mr. Kuhn's signature.

Who's signature is it.

MR. KUHN: That's mine.

MR. ROSENBLOOM: Your Honor —

THE COURT: Mr. Rosenbloom, hold on a second.

The information typed in the attachment to the affidavit —

MS. PHAN: Your Honor, may I be heard on that?

That's Karen Van Buten, and again they put Karen down here and they were told that Mr. Kuhn had to sign and be named on the petition.

MR. ROSENBLOOM: "They" who?

MS. PHAN: Court administrator told them that.

MR. ROSENBLOOM: Your Honor, Mr —

THE COURT: Mr. Rosenbloom, I want to hear from you on this, so I'm not cutting you off without your opportunity to be heard, but it can't be today because its after 4:30 and we have court staff that have expectations. Okay. So I need to address that piece of it.

I'm going to allow Mr. Rosenbloom to be heard on that issue, whether he should be able to prevail on a motion to dismiss based on the fact that the affidavit may be, um, lacking in terms of how its with the petition, for lack of a better way to word this.

I think Mr. Rosenbloom might actually be more articulate then I am, so I'm going to let him be heard on it.

I'm going to require Mr. Kuhn to come back because he was named in the petition and in the caption, and although he wasn't specifically disclosed as a witness, I generally treat those names in a caption as being parties as opposed to witnesses and they don't need to be disclosed previously.

We have the issue that was raised again after the recess by you Ms. Phan again asking to excuseded object receive versus for one of your witnesses and that witness was not called today with the intent that you would submit a two-page brief for your legal authority asking to exclude.

Mr. Rosenbloom will have an opportunity to respond to that.

And I'll rule on it then at the beginning of the next hearing so that if in fact one or both of the observers are present on that date and there is still a concern I'll issue a ruling.

And again I'm noting that Mr. Rosenbloom has asked that I not rule again because I've already done so once, but I'll hear from both of you on a two page letter brief.

Now, Ms. Phan.

MR. ROSENBLOOM: I'm just confused, that's a two page letter brief.

THE COURT: On the issue —

MR. ROSENBLOOM: On the public observing or two pages on my motion?

THE COURT: Not on your motion, I'll hear you

orally on your motion.

And, Ms. Phan, if Mr. Rosenbloom can hold himself to half an hour, what kind of time do you think that you'll need to cross Mr. Rosenbloom, cross the witness that we just excused, and any other kind of rebuttal information or testimony?

MS. PHAN: Your Honor, in light of the fact that we have been here four hours, I'll keep it short. I would say 15, 20 minutes, Your Honor.

THE COURT: I'm going to go with February 22 over probably the clerk's —

MS. PHAN: Your Honor?

THE COURT: Yes.

MS. PHAN: I'm sorry, Your Honor, but Mr. Kuhn is — where are you, Mr. Kuhn?

MR. KUHN: Taiwan.

MS. PHAN: February 22 he's going to be flying from February 19th until March 3rd.

MR. ROSENBLOOM: Your Honor, as of March 8th its likely I'll be in training in the correctional law enforcement capacity for eight weeks, so I wouldn't be available after March 8th, at least for six weeks.

THE COURT: The date that you're leaving, Mr. Kuhn, is?

MR. KUHN: The 19th.

MS. PHAN: February 19th?

THE COURT: What's everybody doing Friday morning?

MR. ROSENBLOOM: Which Friday morning are you talking about.

THE COURT: This coming Friday.

MS. PHAN: I have a speaking engagement, Your Honor, this Friday.

THE COURT: This coming Friday? The other options is next Wednesday in the morning.

THE CLERK: At 10:00 a.m.

THE COURT: At 10:00 a.m. I prefer Wednesday just because its here and the files are here and it's easier for me to keep track of things, but I don't want this going into March.

MR. ROSENBLOOM: If that would give Counsel time to

write her two page brief and my time to respond, I'll come Friday if it would give her enough time then. I'm trying to be kind of her schedule.

THE COURT: Next Wednesday at 10:00 works, then I'm willing to relax written arguments as to the open hearing and you can make your argument for five minutess before we start.

MR. ROSENBLOOM: Okay.

THE COURT: You wouldn't either one have the benefit of knowing what the other will say, on the other hand I think both of you have a pretty good idea of what your position is, so if you're willing to waive a written argument you could make an oral one on Wednesday at 10:00 and probably have at least an hour for you to be able to wrap this up.

MS. PHAN: February 15 ten o'clock Your Honor is that the date I'll make it work.

THE COURT: Yes.

MR. ROSENBLOOM: February 15th, 10:00 o'clock.

THE COURT: That's correct. Mr. Kuhn, are you able to be here.

MR. KUHN: Yes, thank you for accommodating my schedule.

THE COURT: You're welcome. All right, so the matter is continued to Wednesday, February 15th, 2006 at 10:00 o'clock.

If either side discovers a conflict it had better be a really good conflict because as of that date I want to conclude this hearing.

And is there anything further, Mr. Rosenbloom, that we need to address?

10

MR. ROSENBLOOM: Yes, Your Honor. The last time we were here we mentioned personal property at Job Corps that had not been returned, and I think we had talked about up know that property being returned to me. Its been since December, I have a photo that was given to me by my mom who passed away.

THE COURT: Hold on —

MR. ROSENBLOOM: — any ways, its still my property they have not returned from December.
THE COURT: On Wednesday one way or another we'll get to that piece and even if it means Court staff leaves and we sit down and figure out what happens to person property, it will get taken care of.
MS. PHAN: I'll bring it personally from my office.
THE COURT: Then we'll see if its personally here on Wednesday. If not, I'll hear from Mr. Rosenbloom. Have a seat in the waiting area because you have to be served with a copy of the continuance. Until that time this order does remain in full force and effect, Mr. Rosenbloom, so stay away from the Job Corps Center until we can complete the hearing.
MR. ROSENBLOOM: Thank you, Your Honor.
MS. PHAN: One last issue, Your Honor, I ask that Mr. Rosenbloom produce whatever exhibit he intends to introduce. Its only fair so I know what it is.

THE COURT: If you have an exhibit, Mr. Rosenbloom, that you're going to be introducing, if you would provide a copy of it to Counsel so she has it ahead of time.
MR. ROSENBLOOM: Likewise anything she plans to introduce.
THE COURT: I'll make it an across-the-board order, if either of you have anything that you intend to introduce that you haven't disclosed to date, disclose it or it will be excluded if not given to the other person before you come in the door. All right. Thank you. Don't leave without the order.
(Adjourn)

Lucky Rosenbloom welcomes reader responses to 612-661-0923, or email him at l.rosenbloom@yahoo.com

Opinion 25

Democrats block Black vote in Minnesota

Eighty percent of Minnesotans favor requiring a photo ID to vote. This is an overwhelming majority. The Minnesota Democrats failed to pass this legislation.

The Democrats blocked the bill, and the Black legislative Democrats must be held accountable for allowing this to happen. Indiana enjoyed record voter turnout after enacting a photo ID requirement to vote.

If legislators intend to defy the will of their constituents, they are at least obligated to provide evidence that people will be disenfranchised. Democrats could not provide this fact; they switched to using seniors as the new scapegoats to deny Black voting in the subterfuge.

Our election system is full of holes that undermine public confidence in the outcome of our elections. Most often we see this in the Black community. Requiring the use of Minnesota identification, as opposed to a stupid utility bill, would have empowered the Black vote in areas outside of the urban districts.

Every eligible Black voter deserves to have the confidence that his or her vote will not be undermined by a system left wide open to potential errors and abuse.

The voter ID bill will empower and enfranchise the disaffected by providing a free ID to people who don't have one and can't afford one. It's nearly impossible to function in modern society without an ID.

The double standard for unverified same-day registrations and verified advance registrations violates the concept of equal protection under the law and is socially unjust. We must ask ourselves as Black people the reason Democrats wanted nothing to do with voter identification at the voting locations throughout Minnesota.

Many improper voter registrations are rejected only after that voter's ballot has been cast and counted. It can take up to six months to verify the legitimacy of a same-day voter registration. I have seen Blacks leave the voting place because of no utility bill. How many of you carry a doggone utility bill in your pocket?

The Democrats voted against voter identification because it was introduced by Republicans. The Democrats put a serious hurt on the Black community to simply flex their newly gained power. We must ask what Reps. Bobby Champion and Jeff Hayden are going to do about this wickedness from members of their own party.

After Reconstruction to the 1964 Voting Rights Act, Blacks and women have fought hard to augment our right to vote. The Democrats diminished that right by voting down a bill that would have empowered the voting of Blacks and women.

Testifying in front of Democrats for this bill allowed me to feel what it must have been like for Blacks to testify and fight Democrats like Gov. George Wallace and Bull Conner who were against the Civil Rights Movement and voting rights for Blacks. Wallace and Conner would have been proud of the performance of each Democrat that voted the voter ID bill down.

Lucky Rosenbloom welcomes reader responses to 612-661-0923, or email him at l.rosenbloom@yahoo.com

Opinion 26

Should we thank Obama for fewer Blacks in prison?

Recent drug war statistics would have us believe that fewer Blacks are going to prison for drug dealing. Please. Will someone tell the local police and folks in corrections this? To hear some of these professionals tell it, one would think Black men continue to fill up the prisons for dealing crack in high numbers.

We owe it all to Obama being elected the first Black president. However, the media will keep the recent statistics on the down low, not giving brother Obama his props.

The United States drafted a bunch of people 20 years ago and gave them an ongoing mission known as fighting the war on drugs. Because of Obama's presence, the number of Blacks dealing crack and going to prison has decreased. Get this: The number of Whites going to prison for the same crime has increased. Now we will have to wait and see if the tough laws relevant to convictions and sentencing will change.

Look up the Washington Based Sentencing Project report and you will find that the number of Black inmates in prison for drug offenses had fallen from 145,000 in 1999 to 113,000 in 2005, which is about a 21 percent decline. By now, some of you have caught my humor realizing that Obama has nothing to do with this, but it has to be because of the Twin Cities' own superstar Prince, as the drop started in 1999. Thanks, Prince.

You see, the Whites started listening to metal music and partying like rock stars instead of partying like it was 1999. The Whites during the same period rose from 50,000 to more than 72,000 according to the report, showing a 42 percent increase. Ask yourself why we have not seen these numbers plastered all over the liberal media television.

Leave it to me, the fabulous one, the one who is 99 percent right — that one percent was because of advise given to me from an advisor, thus messing up my being right 100 percent of the time. Sorry.

Back to the reason: It's not because of Obama but because prosecutors and law enforcement are more focused on what is destroying their own neighborhoods — methamphetamines. Sorry, Obama. It should not be too difficult finding something to give you credit for with respect to changing the lives of Black men.

Obama and change

I am going to send a letter to President Obama. Dear President Obama, liberals are always raising taxes on Americans, including the Black men. It's already hard enough for a brother to make ends meet without having to pay more taxes that you preached about during your campaign.

I know why you Democrats in the White House want to raise taxes. It's because you all don't pay your taxes. Mr. President, all we have to do is look at several of your appointments that did not pay high taxes and did so only after getting busted.

Now, this conservative voted for you, sir. For my vote, I am asking you to get off this change theme. The way you keep raising taxes, I prefer some bills, some tens, twenties, fifties, a few hundreds. Keep the change, please. The cents are likely not to do us any good having to pay the taxes you Democrats are going to smack us with soon.

Thank you, sir, for reading my letter. I shall wait for your response.

The BCC

Black Cops Capitulate, now known as the BCCs. I can't understand the reasons for five Black cops in the city of Minneapolis, in the great state of Minnesota, giving in to the liberal city council and settling a lawsuit for $740,000.

Five brothers brought a discrimination lawsuit against the city, the police department, and its chief, Tim Dolan. What did the police department have to hide? What did the liberal city council not want us to know? No way would you settle a suit if you had the evidence to show that no such discrimination occurred.

But if you were afraid, if you did not want the truth and nothing but the truth to come out, one would say to others, "Hey, hey, hey, we could be caught lying in depositions, interrogatories and other types of discovery. If they use *subpoena duces tecum*, they could get specified documents and other physical evidence. We have a lot to hide. Settle now."

What did the liberals not want us to know? Why settle if there is nothing to hide? It's like admitting guilt. I would expect a fight out of five Black cops. Wouldn't you?

I fight for my rights because of the desire to have young Black men and women see a real Black man in a world where he is not afraid to stand up for himself. The Black officers giving up is not the message to send in the day of a Black president. Black people must not see this weak-a** settlement as some kind of Black pride and new image.

Lucky Rosenbloom welcomes reader responses to 612-661-0923, or email him at l.rosenbloom@yahoo.com

Opinion 27

Liberals, high taxes destroying the Black family

Because of high taxes and government regulations, Black mothers cannot find affordable housing in urban neighborhoods. Let me tell you how the formula works.

It's simple: Property taxes are going up, and this, matched with landlord regulations, equals high rental rates because the owners have to cover property taxes and the costs of regulations such as added repairs and/or stratifying housing codes.

All over the country, even here in our city, we see Blacks being forced out of their homes because of high property taxes, taxes on items needed for basic survival, and taxes on items needed just to live out your daily lives — not to mention death taxes.

Blacks just chill as Democrats talk about raising taxes. Minnesota is one of the highest taxed states; however, Blacks do nothing to block liberal Democrats from raising taxes, or taking money out of your check to cover deadbeat programs that do not work.

Look at your paycheck. Add up the amount of taxes taken out of your paycheck, each paycheck, monthly. Ask yourself a question: What else could I have done with that $600 or more dollars? You could have made a home payment, a car payment, or covered some pressing bill that threatens your livelihood.

Blacks need to say to the liberal Democrats, "Enough is enough." Tell them their liberal spending and high taxes are destroying the Black family. Tell Democrats how much money is taken out of your paycheck and what you could have done with that income.

Ask them, "Why are you going to raise taxes even more? Why are you going to take even more out of my check, adding to the struggle of my family?"

It's wrong for anyone to blame Republicans for the amount of money that is taken out of your paycheck. If it was left up to Republicans, you would have 60 percent of your taxed income returned. Think about that fact.

How much is taken out of your check to have 60 percent that would not be taken? What could you do with that money? Save for retirement? Buy that new car? Put money in the bank for the education of your children?

Historically, Democrats have always subjected Blacks to unfair tax practices. After the Civil War, tax laws were passed that made it impossible for the Black family to survive, not to mention the Black individual.

Tax laws were passed that pushed Blacks to pay poll taxes and occupation taxes. These taxes kept the Black man and the Black family in chains and were very hurtful, very evil, because they kept the freed slave family from gaining on the White Southern Democrat both economically and educationally.

Today, for Blacks to compete in society we must again be economically and educationally competitive. High taxes are a tool used today to keep the Black man and woman in check. After slavery, if Blacks did not pay poll and occupation taxes, by operation of law they would be arrested and forced into labor.

Blacks must join hands and create another Negro spiritual. The lyrics could be something like: "Democrats, listen to me as you take a legislative break, please do not raise taxes only to have us hurt by the money you will take.

"Oh, Democrat, taking food off my table is a joy that you feel, every time we have to cut back on our Black family meal.

"I am a loyal Democrat you must agree, but do not raise my taxes, or to the Republicans you will lose me.

"Now, you can have me join the Republican Band, or stop taking my money out of my paycheck, leaving more in my hand."

Reality check: local liberal mayors and city council members are talking about raising taxes in order to have more police and firefighters on the street, which would include other City employment. With your hard-earned tax dollars, how many of these people hired will be people of color?

Liberals will take more of your money to create jobs for their relatives and Whites. In tough times, Blacks will pay more to support White liberal families, while the Black family suffers during this poor economy. I'll bet some of you are agreeing with me now.

WARNING: Be on the lookout for terms and/or words such as "fee," or "public options," all sneaky words for raising taxes.

Gotta go and pay my October property taxes now.

Lucky Rosenbloom welcomes reader responses to 612-661-0923, or email him at l.rosenbloom@yahoo.com

Opinion 28

Expect more closet racists to act out

If I am a racist, I'm moving to Rochester, Minnesota. This is the message racists will get if nothing happens to stop or at least condemn the Ku Klux Klan and skinheads that are a part of or are hearing about bias crime in Rochester.

My research has shown a rise in hate crimes in Rochester over the last few years, including a recent incident when a Black woman told police that someone had spray-painted a swastika on her mailbox. The sister would later find similar racist writings painted on laundry walls in her apartment building.

Let me mention as well the two White men in Rochester on trial for second-degree unintentional murder in connection with the beating death of a Somali man, which some Whites in Rochester refuse to recognize as a hate crime.

I have reports of Blacks indicating they are being discriminated against in public schools, public accommodations, and housing in Rochester. In response, the Council on Black Minnesotans Rochester Committee, which I chair, has sent certified letters to several officials asking them to join a focus group to deal with the growing level of hate and bias crimes that most agrees are directed at Rochester's citizens of color.

Letters have been mailed to Sen. Lynch, Congressman Walz, Rochester School Board Chair Ms. Seveson, Rochester City Council Members Wojcik and Means, Rep. Liebling, the director of Rochester's Chamber of Commerce, Rochester's police chief, County Commissioner Perkins, St. Paul Human Rights Commissioner Korbel, Ms. Hocker of Rochester's Diversity Council, Ms. Graves of Rochester's NAACP, and others.

I will keep you up to date on any responses and the development of this focus group should it come together. One hopes that the people to whom these letters were mailed would have a vested concern with inclusiveness in Rochester.

Racist graffiti at Lake Como

Plan a day of fishing at Como Park in St. Paul and you may notice on your favorite fishing bridge racist writings aimed at Blacks. You may also notice the phrase "Kill Obama."

Yes, these hateful expressions were found at Lake Como in St. Paul recently. I've stated before and I shall state this again: Closet racists are going to act out more because they cannot stand the fact that Obama is our president.

This fact compels the closet racist to step out in the dark of night (because laws prohibits them from stepping out with hoods hiding their faces) and leave flyers on your car windows, or write such hate expressions at a family park.

This type of behavior ought to be an embarrassment to White people. What's worse is that most good White people will sit back and do nothing, similar to slavery. Whites knew slavery and lynchings were wrong, but they were afraid to act against it until Republican Lincoln made it popular to do so.

So, here we are again, the racist Whites acting out and Blacks stepping forward attacking this type of hate. Be it Rochester or in our own backyard, racism continues in America.

Anyone who believes that racism is archaic because of Obama being elected president is someone who has the most brilliant mind of the 15th century. I tell you to look for more closet racists to step out and save America using the fear of Obama.

I want to ask you a question: Because I write about racism as I do, does this mean I am racist?

Lucky Rosenbloom welcomes reader responses to 612-661-0923, or email him at l.rosenbloom@yahoo.com

Opinion 29

Lucky Rosenbloom, not a lawyer, prevails against
Minnesota Attorney General Lawyer

You can read the transcript as the hearing happened.

STATE OF MINNESOTA DISTRICT COURT
COUNTY OF RAMSEY SECOND JUDICIAL DISTRICT
——————————————— File No. 62-CV-09-8172

Lucky Rosenbloom,
Plaintiff,
vs.
Lisa Jones and Kevin Lindsey, as agents and Board members of the State of Minnesota, d/b/a Minnesota Counsel on Black Minnesotans,

MOTION HEARING
Defendants.

————————————————————————

The above-entitled matter came duly on for hearing before the Honorable M. Michael Monahan, Judge of District Court, on the 12th day of August 2009, in Courtroom 1580, Ramsey County Courthouse, in the city of St. Paul, state of Minnesota.

APPEARANCES:
Lucky Rosenbloom, appeared pro se.
P. Kenneth Kohnstamm, Esquire, appeared on behalf of the Defendants.

RAMSEY COUNTY DISTRICT COURT
SECOND JUDICIAL DISTRICT
2

THE COURT: Appearances, please.
MR. ROSENBLOOM: My name is Maryland Lucky Rosenbloom, plaintiff.
THE COURT: You're appearing pro se, correct?
MR. ROSENBLOOM: Yes, Your Honor.
MR. KOHNSTAMM: Your Honor, Ken Kohnstamm, K-O-H-N-S-T-A-M-M, for the Attorney General's office for the defendants.
THE COURT: We're here on a motion by the defense to stay discovery in this matter until such time as their motion to dismiss the complaint can be heard and decided. This is an action apparently — well, it's difficult to tell what the action is because the summons and complaint has not been filed by the

plaintiff. I don't believe, Mr. Rosenbloom, you've paid the filing fees, have you?
MR. ROSENBLOOM: No, Your Honor. I believe the rules allow for the complaint to be served and discovery to start, and I believe also allows reasonable time to file that summons and complaint, which I do plan to do within that reasonable time.
THE COURT: Let me tell you what I think just on that point, Mr. Rosenbloom. The rules require that the documents be promptly served and

RAMSEY COUNTY DISTRICT COURT
SECOND JUDICIAL DISTRICT

3

filed, and if I'm reading this thing correctly, you started this thing in February/early March, so it's been five months, more or less, since you started the litigation and still no filing fees, still no filing of the complaint and summons, yeah? We have a budget crisis going on, you know. We can't operate this thing without our filing fees, among other things.
MR. ROSENBLOOM: Absolutely, Your Honor. I was planning —
THE COURT: I think with respect to that, I'm going to let you have 15 days to get that accomplished, and if it's not filed within 15 days, all the fees paid, whatever it is, you need to get yourself up to date, yeah, then we're going to administratively dismiss the case and you're going to have to start all over again.
MR. ROSENBLOOM: Thank you, Your Honor. That was my plan.
THE COURT: That will take care of that portion of the problem.
So, as I understand it here, Mr. Rosenbloom has noticed deposition of at least one or two of the defendants. He wants to take those depositions, apparently, on videotape.
MR. KOHNSTAMM: Correct. He's noticed

RAMSEY COUNTY DISTRICT COURT
SECOND JUDICIAL DISTRICT

4

three depositions. One of the deponents is a named defendant.

THE COURT: Then I must have misread that, but in any event, the notion by the defense is that they have a good motion to dismiss based on the deficiencies in the complaint, as they see it, and the law with respect to a possible immunity of the defendants under state law, and I guess, on balance, they ought not to be put through the exercise of defending against discovery until those Rule 12 motions are decided. Is that more or less it?

MR. KOHNSTAMM: That's it.

THE COURT: What else do you want to tell me about that?

MR. KOHNSTAMM: Three things, Your Honor, very quickly. The court's got broad discretion under Rule 26 to grant the stay that we've requested. We cited the court to the case law that indicates other trial courts have been upheld in their exercise of such discretion, and that the stay we're requesting serves justice and judicial economy. Parties shouldn't be put through the time and expense of videotaped depositions if there is a Rule 12 motion pending, which is scheduled before you October 22nd. Mr. Rosenbloom would not be prejudiced by this inability to do

RAMSEY COUNTY DISTRICT COURT
SECOND JUDICIAL DISTRICT

5

discovery because the only questions come October will be questions of law, not questions of fact, and so for those reasons, we ask the protective order issue.

MR. ROSENBLOOM: Thank you, Your Honor. First of all, I want to respond directly to the memorandum issued to the court by the defendant — or defense. I'd like to start with a question. My question is has the Attorney General's office ever served a complaint and started discovery in a manner in which I'm doing? The answer is probably yes. And now they're here today arguing against something that they have done procedurally themselves. I'm a pro se litigant, obviously this is the Attorney General's office —

THE COURT: But you're not without experience.

MR. ROSENBLOOM: Yes, but if I may finish?

THE COURT: But just to finish out that thought, you are a pro se litigant but not without experience.

MR. ROSENBLOOM: Thank you.

THE COURT: Okay.

MR. ROSENBLOOM: And even though I'm a pro se litigant, I know the court would not weigh more

RAMSEY COUNTY DISTRICT COURT
SECOND JUDICIAL DISTRICT

6

in favor of the Attorney General's office because I've been a pro se litigant.

The cases that he cited are full of the court may, the court may. It doesn't say the court shall. Again, the Attorney General's office themselves have served a complaint and they've started discovery similar to what I'm doing today, and now they're asking you to hold off on something that they've done themselves. The complaint was served; that starts the lawsuit; the rules allow for discovery.

The defendant, in his own motion to the court, has failed to show what the embarrassment would be, what their annoyance would be, what the oppression would be, what the undue burden would be. The complaint was properly served. I have a right to discovery.

The only good cause that I think the defense attorney is saying to the court today is basically we just don't want to do it right now. He hasn't shown a good cause to the court. In his own memorandum, where is the embarrassment? Where is the oppression? Where is the undue burden? Where is the good cause? He hasn't shown that to the court. I haven't heard it. I don't think the court has heard it.

Our discovery is tomorrow. He hasn't even

RAMSEY COUNTY DISTRICT COURT
SECOND JUDICIAL DISTRICT
7

notified, Your Honor, his clients about the discovery for tomorrow. If I had done something like that, Your Honor, and I was before this court and I didn't even notify anyone of discovery for tomorrow and I wasn't planning on participating, they would probably be asking for sanctions, and the court would probably grant it.

There's an issue here, Your Honor, of fairness. I'm sure the court is aware of other attorneys, and even probably pro se litigants like myself, who have served complaints and the court has allowed discovery pending a motion to dismiss. There's no undue burden. The depositions will probably last no longer than 20 minutes per person tomorrow. I think it's pretty much disrespectful, Your Honor, to the process when the attorney has not even notified his client of a deposition tomorrow. There's no good cause here, Your Honor.

THE COURT: Well, what would be the harm to you, Mr. Rosenberry (sic), if the order was granted?

MR. ROSENBLOOM: Are you asking me, Your Honor?

THE COURT: Uh-huh.

MR. ROSENBLOOM: I'm sorry. What was

RAMSEY COUNTY DISTRICT COURT
SECOND JUDICIAL DISTRICT
8

the question?

THE COURT: What prejudice would you suffer if the stay was granted?

MR. ROSENBLOOM: I think I would suffer prejudice in that I filed my complaint, and my complaint is in good faith, and it's possible that with that deposition, that could prevent this case from being dismissed based on the deposition, which also would mean that would deny me my opportunity to even probably file for a summary judgment. So, I have certain things that I'm entitled to that I will be denied just based on a 20-minute deposition.

THE COURT: Yes, is that it, Mr. Rosenbloom?

MR. ROSENBLOOM: Yes, sir.

MR. KOHNSTAMM: Nothing further, Your Honor.

THE COURT: All right. Well, first an observation just off the point, and that is that once again, this is a good example of why Minnesota is 150 years behind the times, if not 800 years behind the times, allowing litigation to commence without proper filing. It's absolutely inexplicable why the state of Minnesota permits that. Indeed, I'm absolutely amazed that Ms. Swanson isn't at the legislature demanding

RAMSEY COUNTY DISTRICT COURT
SECOND JUDICIAL DISTRICT
9

that that particular rule, the only one of two states in the nation that permits such nonsense, continues to be the law in Minnesota. It's absolutely inexplicable, especially in view of the budget crisis that apparently we're all involved in, to allow people to litigate without paying for their writ, to quote Henry the 2nd, and without court supervision, but that's an aside. We've taken care of that here earlier with my observations to Mr. Rosenbloom about filing his complaint.

Moving on, I have to agree with Mr. Rosenbloom that I don't see in here any prejudice to the defendants articulated other than the cost and annoyance of going forward with litigation before their motion to dismiss is heard. And on the other hand, I really don't hear any prejudice to the plaintiff if the stay was granted, so I'm at a loss, frankly, to understand what we're doing here. On the one hand, the expense doesn't seem to be, to me, to be so outrageous or in such a great amount that it would cause a hardship to the defendants, and on the other hand, Mr. Rosenbloom has waited eight months before triggering discovery, and I don't see why waiting a few more months would cause him any prejudice. So, on balance, I'm going to deny the motion

RAMSEY COUNTY DISTRICT COURT
SECOND JUDICIAL DISTRICT

10

for a protective order. Now, I'm worried, though, about why it is we're waiting until October to hear this motion to dismiss. How did that come about?
MR. ROSENBLOOM: Your Honor, I believe it came about after I served my notice for deposition.
THE COURT: I don't — I'm talking about the scheduling. How did we pick October for that?
MR. KOHNSTAMM: It was the earliest date I could —
THE COURT: Get from the scheduling people?
MR. KOHNSTAMM: Yes. I understood that the court was going to be on vacation or unavailable for a substantial chunk of time between now and then, and, of course, I have to serve a brief on Mr. Rosenbloom 28 days in advance.
THE COURT: So let's see if we can straighten that out before you two leave and see if we can get an earlier date for that motion to dismiss.
MR. ROSENBLOOM: So from my understanding, the depositions continue or not?
THE COURT: Yeah, the motion for a

protective order was denied. I don't know what you're

RAMSEY COUNTY DISTRICT COURT
SECOND JUDICIAL DISTRICT

11

going to do, but that's it. I found that there hasn't been a sufficient showing of harm or embarrassment to the defense, and I can't find, equally, that there's been anything shown by the plaintiff to indicate prejudice, so, on balance, we're stuck with the status quo, such as it is.
Mr. Clerk, what kind of dates do we have?
THE CLERK: It's October 22nd, and in order to serve the brief, I don't think we can move it up.
THE COURT: We can't move it up?
THE CLERK: I don't think we can.
THE COURT: Tell me, Mr. Rosenbloom, how you're going to be conducting these particular depositions.
MR. ROSENBLOOM: I'll be conducting the depositions, I'm planning on videotaped deposition.
THE COURT: Where's all of that going to occur?
MR. ROSENBLOOM: It's going to be, as I served notice, it's going to be at Depo International in Minneapolis. I don't have it in front of me right now, but I have the court reporter, everything set up through Depo International.
THE COURT: What time is all this going

RAMSEY COUNTY DISTRICT COURT
SECOND JUDICIAL DISTRICT

12

to happen?
MR. ROSENBLOOM: I believe it was scheduled for 12:00 tomorrow.
MR. KOHNSTAMM: Your Honor, contrary to what was said to the court, I have — my folks all know —
THE COURT: I'm not worried about that.

MR. ROSENBLOOM: He told me today that he hadn't talked to them.

MR. KOHNSTAMM: They knew about this motion, so whether they're all available tomorrow, I don't honestly know. They know this is scheduled for tomorrow, and they know that we were seeking a stay today.

THE COURT: Here's my problem, gentlemen. I'm very leery of videotaped depositions, to start off with. I'm leery of depositions conducted by pro se litigants, secondarily, and I'm particularly leery about this particular deposition given the allegations that I have read in the copy of the complaint that was attached to the motions here.

MR. ROSENBLOOM: Your Honor, as a compromise, I'll —

THE COURT: Hang on, let me finish, and then we'll get back to you. And so I have at least in

RAMSEY COUNTY DISTRICT COURT
SECOND JUDICIAL DISTRICT

13

mind the possibility that this deposition-taking process may need some supervision, and so having that in the back of my head, I'm going to be available tomorrow around noontime by telephone, Mr. Clerk, in case things don't go as smoothly as they might during the course of the depositions. Mr. Rosenbloom, yeah? If things don't go smoothly, then we're going to close down that process and we're going to find someone to help the process along by being there and supervising the conduct of the depositions, or, of course, you all could agree to do that between yourselves, but now, then, you were going to say?

MR. ROSENBLOOM: I'm sorry. I misspoke. I was going to compromise because I thought the concern was videotaped deposition. I was going to compromise and say I won't have a videotaped deposition, I'll just have a deposition, but that wasn't the issue, so I apologize. I was trying to work with —

THE COURT: Yeah, it's cheaper not to have the videotape people there. If there's problems with scheduling, yes, and you can't work that out, then I'm available to help with that process also.

So, two things I'm concerned about; that is, that the depositions, whatever they do, go forward in a

RAMSEY COUNTY DISTRICT COURT
SECOND JUDICIAL DISTRICT

14

reasonable and professional manner without difficulties. And, two, that the scheduling be appropriate for the potential witnesses; that we accommodate their reasonable schedules.

All right. We're in recess.

(At this time another matter was heard.)

RAMSEY COUNTY DISTRICT COURT
SECOND JUDICIAL DISTRICT

15

STATE OF MINNESOTA)
) ss. CERTIFICATE
COUNTY OF RAMSEY)

I, Holly Nordahl, do certify that I am an official court reporter in and for the County of Ramsey, Second Judicial District, State of Minnesota, and that I reported the foregoing proceedings in this matter, and that the transcript contained on the foregoing 14 pages is a true and correct transcript of the shorthand notes taken by me at the said time and place herein mentioned.

DATED: August 31, 2009.

/s/______________________________

HOLLY NORDAHL, RPR, CRR
Official Court Reporter
15 West Kellogg Boulevard
St. Paul, Minnesota 55102
Telephone: (651)266-9185

RAMSEY COUNTY DISTRICT COURT
SECOND JUDICIAL DISTRICT

Lucky Rosenbloom welcomes reader responses to 612-661-0923, or email him at l.rosenbloom@yahoo.com

Opinion 30

St. Paul Urban League wants my money

But I think I'll keep my $25 for now

Read up on this! The St. Paul Urban League (which never contacts me for anything) suddenly contacted this columnist to attend some kind of an event. I was told to bring money and give my bucks upon entering.

Well, operating on the benefit of the doubt, I prepared my check in the amount requested and preceded to the Urban League. The Luckster was driving down Selby on my motorcycle, saving gas by not driving my SUV, allowing me to write out that $25 check — and I was met by protesters. Yes, protesters, protesting the St. Paul Urban League.

You all know me. I smelled a story, something to get others' opinions about. So, I asked a few protesters, "Why protest an event at the Urban League in St. Paul?"

Here we go.

"Mr. Lucky," says D.B., "from my standpoint the St. Paul Urban League has slowly but surely diminished right in front of my eyes, and apparently many others like me. I was referred to S.P.U.L. on several occasions and decided to try to take advantage of its services only to find out that there were none.

"They had no employment or services posted on the bulletin board. No employees to help with questions. Then I went to use their so-called resource room that only consisted of four computers, one of which looked so outdated that it's probably considered an antique.

"Why is it they would only have these computers when they were granted thousands of dollars for new computers for the public?" D.B. continued. "Where is the money going? It's very obvious for anyone to notice even from the outside looking in that whoever the director of this chapter is need not be in that position.

"I recently found out at a rally of the people and former employees that the man who pulled up in the new Mercedes Benz was Scott Selmer, the director there of two years. He's the person...who in only two years transformed an organization of integrity for 40-plus years for the public into a memory of what it once was.

"Please help save the St. Paul Urban League and get us new and honest leadership. It's time for change!"

This columnist talked to another protester named L.R., who asked, "Why is this agency being allowed to perish? Mr. Selmer needs to step down so that this agency can be revived. Why won't he face the community and answer direct questions? This agency and the community deserve to have competent leadership."

"I challenge Mr. Selmer to answer the question, 'Do you have a vested interest in this agency and this community?' I ask the board to step up to the plate and do the right thing...

"Mr. Selmer blames United Way for the downfall of the agency. United Way does not run this agency. Mr. Selmer does," said L.R. "Why has Mr. Selmer not been held accountable for the state that the agency is in and the part he plays in that? You look at his track record and decide for yourselves. I say we deserve better!"

This columnist, feeling he was on a roll, asked another protester named K.C. to comment. "This past Saturday," K.C. said, "I and a few others from the great Saint Paul community held a protest against the Saint Paul Urban League. Never in a day did I think I would have to stand against a historical African American organization.

"Let me be very clear — it is not the Urban League that we stand against, but its current leadership, lack of presence in the community, and no response as to why that is! I have heard from my elders in the Rondo community that the Saint Paul Urban League was once a thriving force in the community.

"As a former employee of the Urban League, I have heard over and over that the issue is funding. I do understand the importance of funding in the nonprofit sector, especially during such uncertain economic times; however, funding is not the only source that keeps the doors open.

"Leadership is an important part of it, as well as proof of how the community is being served. There have been a few articles circulating regarding the issue with the Saint Paul Urban League. One can find these sources in the September's *Insight* and *Spokesman-Recorder*.

"I attempted to get answers during the protest from a Sgt. Jefferson, whom I believe is the chair of the board and a well-respected member of the Saint Paul community. Once again, it was stated that the issue is funding.

"I asked about the responsibility of Scott Selmer, whom the board put in place as executive director. To no avail — I received the silent treatment. I informed the sergeant that during my brief stay with the Saint Paul Urban League, I found my experience working under Mr. Selmer extremely unpleasant. In my eight years of serving the community and working in the nonprofit sector, I have never seen such disarray.

"The mission of the Saint Paul Urban League," said K.C. "is to assist African Americans and other culturally diverse groups in the achievement of social and economic equality. This great mission is not being followed or respected, so I call on communities of all cultures and geographical areas to stand in solidarity to get the Saint Paul Urban League back on its feet and under new leadership!

"As I stated earlier, it saddens me to have to display in this manner what has taken place with this historical organization, but *we have to hold our own accountable at times!"*

For now, this columnist will keep his $25.

Lucky Rosenbloom welcomes reader responses to 612-661-0923, or email him at l.rosenbloom@yahoo.com

Opinion 31

Black Alliance for Educational Options backs school choice

The Black Alliance for Educational Options (BAEO) is a national non-profit, nonpartisan organization whose mission is to actively support parental choice to empower families and increase quality educational options for Black Children.

Since 1999, BAEO has emerged as the voice for low-income and working-class Black parents who want access to high quality educational options for their children. BAEO has served more than 10,000 low-income and working-class parents by providing them with the tools they need to select quality schools and supplementary services for their children.

As BAEO's membership grows, so does the proof that our opponents deny: Black people support parental choice and want quality educational options for their children. Our organization has the potential to change the face of the school choice movement by presenting ourselves to political leaders as a substantial constituency of Black choice supporters. A large, strong membership is the most powerful tool BAEO has, to make real changes for our children.

Locally, we hold monthly information meetings on the fourth Tuesday of each month from 6-7 pm at the Center for Families (3333 N. 4th Street, Minneapolis) to introduce people to BAEO. We hold Parent Empowerment Seminars where we teach parents about their child's learning styles, behavioral styles, and how to create a win-win relationship with their child's teacher.

We have held these meetings monthly, but we are interested in holding the seminars for a school or organization that can get a group of parents together. We also take groups to Milwaukee for school tours and discussions with key school choice activists including Dr. Howard Fuller (chairman of BAEO and former superintendent of Milwaukee Public Schools), Ken Johnson (Milwaukee School Board member and former president who ushered in school choice within the district), and Rep. Jason Fields (one of few Black Democratic school choice supporters).

We also advocate for school choice at the legislative via testifying and monitoring education committees. I became a member of BAEO because it was the right thing to do it is up to people like me and like you out there to take a stand and demand quality educational options for all children.

Minnesota has been known for its innovative thinking around education and for being the home to the nation's first chartered school legislation. It's time that we make the connection between academic achievement for all children and the economic future of this nation, state and city.

We must focus on excellence as the standard, no matter race, income or culture. Milwaukee has learned this lesson early. We need you to help in this fight because this is the greatest civil rights issue of our lifetime.

This columnist supports schools choice.

For more information on BAEO, call 612-605-1942 (please dial all 10 digits) or email tiffany@baeo.org. You can also learn more at www.baeo.org. Tiffany Green is one of two BAEO Minnesota project managers as well as the policy aide to Minneapolis City Council Vice President Robert Lilligren.

Lucky Rosenbloom welcomes reader responses to 612-661-0923, or email him at l.rosenbloom@yahoo.com

Opinion 32

Blacks need more faith in self-reliance

I find four concepts that keep Blacks from becoming economically and educationally competitive: 1) double standards, 2) preferential treatment, 3) provisions for cultural differences, and 4) entitlement. As I write in my book Liberal Racism Creates the Black Conservative, the reason other minorities, including people from Africa, come to this great place (America) and augment their lives is because they have not accepted these concepts.

I attended a meeting on October 14, 2008, at the Martin Luther King Center, the subject being economics. I heard people blaming Republicans, Pawlenty, banks, and others for Black failure, including private business.

If my dad (Tiger Jack) begged banks, government, or accepted one of the liberal concepts of doom (see 1-4 above), his tiny store would not have been moved to the Historical Society, and the street would have not been named after him. If he had waited on or begged anyone, he would not be the example of Black hard work without excuses that many have read about, seen news reports about, or visited the Historical Society to learn about.

How can any Black organization preach and/or accept this begging acceptance, and preach the same doomsday theories that have failed our community for years?

I make $900 in five hours (more than some make in a week), plus income from drafting pleadings for lawyers, music from my musical talent, my book, two jobs and other skills. If I had begged government to help me instead of working overtime on several jobs to save money and start my business, I would not be sharing this with you now.

If I had waited for handouts and blamed the White man for holding me back instead of working harder than the other guy, I would not have degrees and education in paralegal, education, law enforcement and social sciences.

Blacks have to let go of those agencies that teach us failure by always depending on government programs to help us start businesses or matriculating into college if we are to be "race competitive" in the coming century. Any agency, any organization that promotes begging or waiting for some kind of handout, for a loan that we blame the White man for not getting, is to promote Black doom with respect to education and economic growth.

Heck, I never got a loan to start my business; I worked hard, overtime, got the money and did it on my own. Yes, just like Tiger Jack. People that wait for the handout, place blame, wait for 1-4, are not doing anything except to hate on me or accuse me of having some kind of silver spoon.

In my book, I promote the idea that performance does not follow self-esteem.

When you refuse to wait on the White man or his agencies, when you work harder than the other guy to get what you want, this allows performance. Performance equals high expectations. High expectations equal self-reliance. Self-reliance equals successful Black business people.

I have attended meetings in the community for over 20 years. I listen to the same old liberal concepts of doom and failure. When are our leaders, the leaders of agencies, including members of the Council on Black Minnesotans, going to learn to stop promoting dependency? Our social programs are left begging for money to serve members of our community. Funding, funding – if we don't get enough, we have to stop this or that. Let's blame Pawlenty.

All the money people say we have in the community, if we truly do spend it outside of our community then we have no one to blame but ourselves.

A story: I know a Black youth who wanted to start a t-shirt business with designs. He could not get a loan and did not know where to turn for help after he had been turned away by agencies. He had accepted concepts 1-4.

I told him to bring me some of his works. He did. After looking at his work, I responded, "You mean to tell me, with all this talent to make money, you are going to wait on someone to give you something to start? Get your butt a job, two jobs, save enough money to buy your supplies, buy your shirts, have some flyers printed."

He did so, now, he has contracts to do business with companies. At times, as he walks by my store, people stop him on the street to do business. He offers me thanks, which I refuse to take. My thanks are seeing him walk by my store with shirts in his hands, saying, "Gotta keep moving, and got to get my orders done."

Black leaders from all agencies must teach self-reliance and get away from this group agency of blame and failure.

Lucky Rosenbloom welcomes reader responses to 612-661-0923, or email him at l.rosenbloom@yahoo.com

Opinion 33

Council on Black Minnesotans must be held to high standards

I appreciated many of you supporting my comments about the Council on Black Minnesotans (COBM) a year ago. My concern was the COBM's many audits, audit after audit that seemed to have the same mistakes over and over.

I would not accept these inadequate daily operations from an organization representing all Blacks and African Americans in Minnesota. While my approbation was cogent, my intent was high standards in the COBM representation of our people and community.

Because of my endless drive contacting legislators, members of the attorney general's office and others, most errors have been corrected and a plan has been presented that will give the auditors no choice but to issue exemplary conclusions with respect to the council's next audit report.

While many of you supported my endeavors, there were those who would send letters to Governor Tim Pawlenty and the attorney general's office in an insipid attempt to have me removed from the COBM Board of Directors. Their efforts proved futile.

The director, Lest Collins, deserves adulation for correcting previous findings and for his development of strategies that will no doubt provide improved future findings that Blacks and African Americans will be proud of. The COBM represents our people, and all of us must hold the COBM to high standards.

Onward Mr. Collins, good job. Now, take the COBM to another level. A revival is in order.

Big money with lots of questions

Let me take a little time to introduce you to some big money. In 1928, we had spenders with large pockets. Trump, Jackson, Cosby and Oprah had nothing on the back-in-the-day rich folks.

Checking the history books, help me figure out which class of folks carried around a $500 bill having the portrait of William McKinley. How about the $1,000 bill with the portrait of Grover Cleveland? My pockets would be burring with a $5,000 bill with the mug of James Madison.

Can you imagine robbing a bank and trying to reduce a $10,000 bill with the smiling face of Salmon Chase? I wonder if Woodrow Wilson got the chance to ask for smaller bills in change for the $100,000 bill with his portrait.

Let us continue to be big-time spenders with $1, $2, $5, $10, $20, and $100 bills. How about a Lucky $70 bill in 2007, with my portrait? Hey, William Jefferson, have any cold cash I may borrow?

The bones of Jesus

Supposedly, some dudes discovered the bones of Jesus in 1980 or so and recently released their findings in this year of 2007. It seems to me that every time we have one of these inconsequential discoveries intended to raise doubt with our Christian beliefs, it only adds documentation to the millions already written about Christ, more than about any other person in the world.

Thus, we must look at all the other religions that have risen and fallen due to these types of discoveries and be amazed that, no matter what the challenges, the Christian movement withstands the test of time.

The birth of racist cartoons

It never fails. Whenever I write something about the Democrats, others will write something about Republicans. Be this in an editorial, another newspaper, or some local cable access program, somewhere someone will write some kind of response not challenging my findings, but with the purpose of writing something wonderful about the Democrats. Please, challenge my findings. So, here we go – follow the leader.

In 1898, our friendly neighborhood Democrats in North Carolina (never talked about today by local Black leaders) had ambition to drive out Black political power despite the number of political officials being at a minimum. (Blacks were elected officials in the Republican Party.) These Democrats implemented an openly racist campaign of White supremacy. This would give birth to the racist cartoons that were vitriolic in substance and depicted Blacks as a threat, with an emphasis them being a threat to White women.

After this implementation of the birth of racist cartoons by the Democrats, we would witness racist drawings in textbooks, magazines, newspapers, and later broadcast media. Yes, we continue to witness evidence of this birth today on the internet, television, and throughout the media. Let us thank the Democrats for this racist birth through the use of cartoons that we continue to deal with today.

This Black conservative is not finished. Democrats would organize groups of racist Democrat murderers calling themselves the "Red Shirts". These people sported red shirts as a symbol that they had killed a Black man. This group of Democrats mobilized to prevent Blacks from voting in North Carolina on election days.

Now, for those White and Black Democrats that have an issue with me for writing this information, I say, don't get mad at me; take up the issue with your history. Democrats have been responsible for many cruelties directed at Black people.

Lucky Rosenbloom welcomes reader responses to 612-661-0923, or email him at l.rosenbloom@yahoo.com

Opinion 34

Black Alliance for Educational Options backs school choice

The Black Alliance for Educational Options (BAEO) is a national non-profit, nonpartisan organization whose mission is to actively support parental choice to empower families and increase quality educational options for Black Children.

Since 1999, BAEO has emerged as the voice for low-income and working-class Black parents who want access to high quality educational options for their children. BAEO has served more than 10,000 low-income and working-class parents by providing them with the tools they need to select quality schools and supplementary services for their children.

As BAEO's membership grows, so does the proof that our opponents deny: Black people support parental choice and want quality educational options for their children. Our organization has the potential to change the face of the school choice movement by presenting ourselves to political leaders as a substantial constituency of Black choice supporters. A large, strong membership is the most powerful tool BAEO has, to make real changes for our children.

Locally, we hold monthly information meetings on the fourth Tuesday of each month from 6-7 pm at the Center for Families (3333 N. 4th Street, Minneapolis) to introduce people to BAEO. We hold Parent Empowerment Seminars where we teach parents about their child's learning styles, behavioral styles, and how to create a win-win relationship with their child's teacher.

We have held these meetings monthly, but we are interested in holding the seminars for a school or organization that can get a group of parents together. We also take groups to Milwaukee for school tours and discussions with key school choice activists including Dr. Howard Fuller (chairman of BAEO and former superintendent of Milwaukee Public Schools), Ken Johnson (Milwaukee School Board member and former president who ushered in school choice within the district), and Rep. Jason Fields (one of few Black Democratic school choice supporters).

We also advocate for school choice at the legislative via testifying and monitoring education committees. I became a member of BAEO because it was the right thing to do it is up to people like me and like you out there to take a stand and demand quality educational options for all children.

Minnesota has been known for its innovative thinking around education and for being the home to the nation's first chartered school legislation. It's time that we make the connection between academic achievement for all children and the economic future of this nation, state and city.

We must focus on excellence as the standard, no matter race, income or culture. Milwaukee has learned this lesson early. We need you to help in this fight because this is the greatest civil rights issue of our lifetime.

This columnist supports schools choice.

For more information on BAEO, call 612-605-1942 (please dial all 10 digits) or email tiffany@baeo.org. You can also learn more at www.baeo.org. Tiffany Green is one of two BAEO Minnesota project managers as well as the policy aide to Minneapolis City Council Vice President Robert Lilligren.

Lucky Rosenbloom welcomes reader responses to 612-661-0923, or email him at l.rosenbloom@yahoo.com

Opinion 35

Liberal taxes continue to hurt Black families

Come on, Democrats, when are you all going to stop the madness of letting rich liberals keep raising our taxes who will not feel the pain themselves? My previous column outlined the real, hard facts about liberals destroying the Black family with taxes. Now, the Democrat liberals will destroy your family in the name of Tim Pawlenty, Governor of Minnesota.

The Democrats running government in Hennepin County in the great state of Minnesota have a very strong ambition to bring down the Black family – okay, I'll throw in the poor and other families of color – by raising property taxes by five percent. You see, the liberal Democrat will always use the poor against the poor, Blacks against Blacks, to justify raising taxes while they, the liberals Democrats, benefit from jobs within our community while living outside our community.

Let me cut to the chase: The intelligent, liberal Democrat will raise your property tax as much as 4.95 percent to help cover the number of uninsured people at the county hospital. These people are using the bad economy as the reason. So, Black homeowners, some who have lost their jobs, are going to struggle even more to cover another poor Black person's hospital bill.

Which one of you will say no to this? The ones to benefit will be liberal Democrats able to keep their jobs at the hospital and other locations, while you are out of a job because of the economy and with higher property taxes, facing foreclosure. Boy, this really helps you out; does it not?

Every elected official in your neighborhood continue to keep their jobs, from Keith Ellison and Amy Klobuchar all the way down to Rybak (your mayor), city council members to county commissioners – they continue to have their homes, yet you do not. You suffer from high taxes that these liberals inflict on you and your babies.

Organize and stop this unfairness. Stop letting the liberal Democrats destroy your Black family. Look at the economy: Things are very hard, yet the liberal Democrats are still raising taxes. It's like they could care less about your family. The Democrats are your worst enemy, not the Republicans.

Ask yourselves why local liberal leaders are allowing this to happen to your family. When you have an answer, let me know. I'll print it in my column.

About President Obama

I like to look back at when people are on the campaign trail making promises that make you feel good.

So good, you want to vote for the person. Well, about the only thing President Obama has accomplished as of 9-11, 2009, is being the best president at ubiquity in history. The man is all over the place.

What he has not done as of this date is get his healthcare reform idea passed. During his campaign Obama promised health care would be available to all Americans, regardless of illness and/or pre-existing conditions. The package he promised would cover all essential medical services, such as maternity.

Guess what? Not done. Obama promised we would be able to move from job to job without penalties or the loss of our current healthcare coverage. As of 9-11, 2009, not so.

At the risk of being called an Uncle Tom, this is feeling kind of good. Let me continue with Obama's campaign promise relating to Iraq. Remove one to two combat brigades monthly. Say it with me: as of 9-11, 2009, not done.

Engage representatives from levels of Iraq society to develop a new accord on Iraq's constitution. Say it with me: as of 9-11, 2009, not done.

What about Obama's promise to start an aggressive diplomatic approach to reach stability in Iraq and the Middle-East? Say it with me: as of 9-11, 2009, not done.

History must record that as of 9-11, 2009, Obama's only real accomplishment is his ability to be ubiquitous. For this, I say come to Minneapolis and put a stop to liberal Democrats raising taxes that destroy Black families. You have the power because you are the ubiquitous one.

Please return my sign

I had a sign at my store in St. Paul that read "President Obama has protection, so should you; get your permit to carry a gun." I was not trying to be humorous by using the president's name that way. It's true, the president has all kinds of protection, but he wants to restrict our rights under the Second Amendment. All I was trying to say is this: Let the president get rid of all his protection; then I will sell my guns and stop teaching the permit-to-carry course.

Just think about the reality of my message, and bring my sign back. Oh, no reward offered.

Lucky Rosenbloom welcomes reader responses to 612-661-0923, or email him at l.rosenbloom@yahoo.com

Opinion 35

More lies my teacher told me

For those of you who believer that Lucky Rosenbloom is the only one that liberal educators lied to, and/or that he did not present all the facts about true Black history and /or Republicans in an effort toward making the Democrats appear as gods to Black people, I asked a Black woman to provide information she never learned in school, starting from grades one through 12.

Frances Rice, chairman of the National Black Republican Association and author of the article, "Why Martin Luther King, Jr. was a Republican," responded to my inquiry with the following abridged version of her views on the subject for publication here:

"It should come as no surprise that Dr. Martin Luther King, Jr. was a Republican. In that era, almost all Black Americans were Republicans because the Republican Party was started in 1854 as the anti-slavery party and was known as the party for Blacks.

Republicans fought to free Blacks from slavery and amended the Constitution to grant Blacks freedom (13th Amendment), citizenship (14th Amendment) and the right to vote (15th Amendment); Republicans passed the civil rights laws of the 1860s, including the Civil Rights Act of 1866 and the Reconstruction Act of 1867.

During the 1960s, it was the Democrats that Dr. King was fighting. Democrat Public Safety Commissioner Theophilus Eugene "Bull" Connor in Birmingham let loose vicious dogs and turned skin-burning fire hoses on Black civil rights demonstrators. Democrat Georgia Governor Lester Maddox famously brandished ax handles to prevent Blacks from patronizing his restaurant.

Democrat Alabama Governor George Wallace stood in front of the Alabama schoolhouse in 1963 and thundered, 'Segregation now, segregation tomorrow, segregation forever.' In 1954, Democrat Arkansas Governor Orville Faubus tried to prevent desegregation of a Little Rock public school.

After Democrat President Franklin D. Roosevelt received the vote of African Americans due to his 'New Deal' appeal and took office in 1933, he rejected both anti-lynching laws and the establishment of a permanent Civil Rights Commission. Democrat President Harry Truman not only rejected Republican efforts to enact anti-lynching laws and establish a permanent Civil Rights Commission, but also failed to enforce his 1948 Executive Order designed to desegregate the military. It was Republican President Dwight Eisenhower who established the Civil Rights Commission, enforced the desegregation of the military, and appointed Chief Justice Earl Warren to the

U.S. Supreme Court, which resulted in the 1954 *Brown vs. Board of Education* decision ending school segregation.

"Democrat President John F. Kennedy voted against the 1957 Civil Rights Act while he was a senator, as did Democrat Senator Al Gore, Sr. Also, after he became president, John F. Kennedy was opposed to the 1963 March on Washington by Dr. King that was organized by A. Philip Randolph, who was a Black Republican. President Kennedy, through his brother Attorney General Robert Kennedy, had Dr. King wiretapped and investigated by the FBI on suspicion of being a Communist in order to undermine Dr. King.

Unknown is the fact that Republican Senator Everett Dirksen from Illinois was key to the passage of civil rights legislation in 1957, 1960, 1964, 1965. Dirksen wrote the language for the 1965 Voting Rights Act. He also crafted the language for the Civil Rights Act of 1968 which prohibited discrimination in housing. President Lyndon Johnson could not have achieved passage of civil rights legislation without the support of Republicans.

Those who wrongly criticize Senator Barry Goldwater for his Libertarian view that the state governments, not the federal government, should enact anti-discrimination laws, ignore President Lyndon Johnson's dismal civil rights record. President Johnson, in his 4, 50-word State of the Union Address delivered on January 4, 1965, mentioned scores of topics for federal action, but only 35 words were devoted to civil rights. He did not mention one word about voting rights.

The statement by President Johnson about losing the South after passage of the 1964 civil rights law was not made out of a concern that racist Democrats would suddenly join the Republican Party that was fighting for the civil rights of Blacks. Instead, it was an expression of fear that the racist Democrats would again form a third party, such as the short-lived States' Rights Democratic Party. In fact, Alabama's Democrat Governor George C. Wallace in 1968 started the American Independent Party that attracted other racist candidates, including Democrat Atlanta Mayor Lester Maddox.

Contrary to the false assertions by Democrats, the racist 'Dixiecrats' did not all migrate to the Republican Party. Regarding the party slogan 'Segregation Forever!', the Dixicrats, who were Democrats, (a) formed the States' Rights Democratic Party for the presidential election of 1948, (b) remained Democrats for all local elections and all subsequent national elections, and (c) declared that they would rather vote for a 'yellow dog' than a Republican, because the Republican Party was known as the party for Blacks.

Democrats expressed little, if any, concern when the racially segregated South voted solidly for Democrats; yet they unfairly deride Republicans because of the 30-year odyssey of the South switching to the Republican Party that began in the 1970s with President Richard Nixon's 'Southern Strategy', which was an effort on the part of Nixon to get Christians in the South to stop voting for Democrats who did not share their values, and who were discriminating against Blacks. Georgia did not switch until 2002, and some Southern states, including Louisiana, are still controlled by Democrats.

Lucky Rosenbloom welcomes reader responses to 612-661-0923, or email him at l.rosenbloom@yahoo.com

Opinion 36

The worries of the Black mother

There was a time when a mother's child was born and if that child would be born male, the mother would have to worry about her son growing up being beaten and/or lynched because of Democrats such as George Wallace and Bull Conner.

Today, a Black mother has a similar worry, but at the hands of other Black males.

When a Black mother has a male child today, she worries about Black thugs or gang members that will shoot and kill her son, or the fear of another Black male shooting one of her girls, that girl being an unintended target.

Talk with a Black mother today about her worries. It's not the police, the KKK or other worries about her male son as in the 1950s and '60s. Its other mother's male children killing her own or others.

What a future we have with Democrats being elected to office.

Americans – this means you – have a lot to look forward to anytime Democrats are elected to serve our people. We may look forward to the best service year after year. In fact, year after year, one can feel the service of elected Democrats letting us know that they continue to work towards improving the quality of life for Black folks. Heck, not only Blacks, but all Americans.

This is what each Democrat running for office should really say in their campaign mumble jumble: "When I become your next whatever, I will create a larger government creating more jobs, which Blacks will not get, and more dependency programs, which Blacks will get. Just to make it fair, to pay for this growth in government and dependency programs, I'll raise your taxes and anything else to keep my people employed and your people dependent on government handouts."

At this moment, the candidate gains applause and don't use the dig-gone thing. "I got your backs by having daycare in schools. So, don't worry, get pregnant, we got your back." More applause.

The candidate again, this time with an added sense of audience esteem, continues, this time without saying thank you. "All you GLBT folks don't worry, your community has gone to $%^^, with gangs, high taxes, no jobs, that we keep promising to do something about.

"Never mind all of this. Why? I'm throwing in my support for gay marriage. As I, your next whatever, become your next whatever, I shall be seated in my nice office, looking out my window and down on your neighborhood, admiring this bright future, I have given you."

"Thanks for your support. Today, at this time, I ask you to look at education, jobs and health care in your community, we – Democrats got your backs on these issues too. Change, change, change: Keep waiting, and remember waiting on government is good for the Black spirit.

"Thanks, for your support. Thank you for your vote. See you at the polls."

Racism today

We all have stories about racism: being followed in some store, or something. I would like to hear your story. If you've experienced racism, or know of a family member that has experienced racism, contact me. Share your story.

Lucky Rosenbloom welcomes reader responses to 612-661-0923, or email him at l.rosenbloom@yahoo.com

Opinion 37

Black gangs share the vision of the KKK

*"Last week, a White man was fined for shooting a rabbit out of season. But of course, it's safe to murder a Negro. A rabbit is better off than a Negro because in Alabama, Ni****s are always in season."*

Vernon Johns

We have Black so-called organized gang members who sell drugs to mothers, fathers and teens in our community, causing drug babies and zombies walking around in our community. Black so-called organized gangs have Black seniors afraid to come out of their homes. These gang members shoot and kill innocent babies and rival gang members in our community.

They are not really organized, because they do not control anything. The same corner they stand on and will shoot another Black person over, they will run like hell from when the police approach them. Law enforcement will clear them off the same corner if the mayor gets tired of them hanging out, or if a business owner wants the land — the same block they would have shot you over if you walked on their territory.

These thugs are not organized. They exist because of some White man living the big life that provides the drugs these thugs sell in our community. While this same man lives the big life, these fools are killing each other and innocent people.

These fools cause problems in our schools preventing other law-abiding Black students from learning. They are like the evil Alabamans Vernon Johns talked about who kept Black people "always in season." They are like the evil devils Malcolm X talked about who would bring drugs into the community of Harlem using Blacks to sell this poison to be injected into the body and spirit of our people.

Yes, my people, Black gangs have become the White Devils Malcolm X talked about. Black gang members have become the KKK of the community.

Like the KKK, Nazis and others who killed our people, we need to stand strong against the new killer of Black babies, men and women, the new threat to our survival. The Black gang members are the Black Devils in our communities and schools that prevent safety and learning in our society.

As Malcolm X would talk about a school system wherein White liberals would pass down the used text books, preventing our children from learning, now they can't learn because of being on drugs sold to them by Black thugs. We need to call these thugs what they are — supporters of the KKK.

Blacks need to stop protecting this new KKK of our community. Blacks need to get together and run them out. Malcolm X would never have tolerated these thugs pushing drugs on our wonderful Black sisters and babies. Black leaders need to deal with these killers in our community as they would if the KKK were responsible for such harmful acts inflicted by Blacks on Blacks.

This is the reason you will not see these kinds of things in White neighborhoods on the scale you see in Black neighborhoods. Whites will support law enforcement when they arrest and/or shoot a thug in self-defense. Black leaders need to send a clear message to law enforcement: Run the new KKK out of our communities.

Other social evils

Malcolm X and Martin Luther King were against killing Black unborn babies. For all of you Black liberals voting for folks promoting abortions, for you Black liberal elected officials promoting abortions, you are the death of our community and the death of the Civil Rights Movement.

After years of Black people being lynched, Black women are raped, Black folks that have disappeared, how is it that you will support or vote for anyone supporting abortion of Black babies? Martin Luther King did win the Margaret Sanger Award (Planned Parenthood) in 1996 for his pro-life position.

I have always stated that the gay rights movement must stand on it's on. I cannot stand gays' attempts to connect gay rights with civil rights. Alveda King, a relative of Martin Luther King, Jr., says, "To equate homosexuals with race is to give a death sentence to civil rights. No one is enslaving homosexuals or making them sit in the back of the bus."

When you vote too liberal, you do so in direct conflict with King and Malcolm. It's time for Blacks to step up to the high standards expressed by Malcolm X, Vernon Johns and Martin Luther King. Black people, we deserve better than the kinds of social evils going on in our communities today. Don't you agree?

Lucky Rosenbloom welcomes reader responses to 612-661-0923, or email him at l.rosenbloom@yahoo.com

Opinion 38

Immigration Law-Absolutely

Double Standards, Racism and Immigration-Not Godly, or Justifiable for America

I shall open this Immigration Prospectus with a powerful anecdote, a story that supports my thesis that there is a casual relationship between racism and Immigration law and its influence in our politics and court system.

Preamble

A white supremacist group rallied against illegal immigration in Los Angeles city centre on April 18, 2010 as hundreds of counter-protesters gathered in a tense standoff that resulted several arrests, thrown rocks and police in riot gear.

Police officers stood between the white supremacists and counter-demonstrators on the south lawn of Los Angeles' City Hall, where about 50 members of the National Socialist Movement waved American flags and swastika banners for about an hour.

The white supremacists, many of them wearing flack helmets and black military fatigue uniforms, shouted 'Sieg Heil' before each of their speakers took the podium to taunt counter-protesters with racial, anti-Semitic and misogynistic epithets.

Let me take you on an historical journey through our United States Supreme Court allowing you to see the influence and motivation of hate groups of yesterday, and hate groups of today with respect to race and immigration laws.

Immigration laws, racism and the courts

I have some serious concerns about immigration laws because the laws are motivated by the Ku Klux Klan and other racist individuals. What is more disturbing is how easy it is for people of the same race and ethnicity to call people looking like them "illegal."

Often, when this happens, I'll ask, what makes that person illegal? To this most respond, "The law says so," or, "These people [which shocks me more, because "these people" are of the same race as the person responding] come over here illegally, while I was born here."

I respond, "What makes a person who looks like you illegal?" Let me admit, the prodding is to lead them into admitting that the law makes them illegal. Getting this desired response, it's time to move into my claims and supporting arguments.

This will be the beginning of my future opinions regarding this concept of illegal immigrants, what make a person illegal, and why. It's so easy for people of the same culture, race and ethnicity to accept their own people as illegal.

Where is a good place to start? With our highest court, the United States Supreme Court. Armed with pen and paper and my Westlaw Library card, it was time to visit the law library to involve myself in some research for some of the darkest decisions relevant to race and the U.S. Supreme Court. Let's get started.

Dread Scott v. Sanford (1856): A slave wanted his freedom; our Supreme Court was not having this (like the Court today, sending back "illegals") and ruled against the Black slave. Added racism is shown when the Court compelled itself to rule that the Bill of Rights did not apply to Blacks, sort of like the Bill of Rights do not apply to "illegals" today.

Here, it was clear to the Court that if the Bill of Rights applied to slaves, these slaves would be allowed liberties of speech in public places, to hold public meetings, keep and carry arms (I wonder what the justices at that time would think about my teaching the permit-to-carry class today), and as you know, today, all this applies to "illegal's."

If one is illegal, one would be afraid to do these things because of being deported. Scary how similar this is, right? The White Court and the Whites they represented found this too horrifying. Well, the idea of "illegal's" coming to America is horrifying to many today.

Pace v. Alabama (1883): Dang. You know we have to have something from the KKK and the courts from Alabama in 1883. If you married outside your race, it had better be a really good relationship with some strong loving going on, because it would mean seven years hard labor in a state penitentiary.

A brother named Tony Pace and a White woman named Mary Cox had the courage to challenge this law. The Supreme Court put the couple back in their place by giving the opinion that the law was race-neutral. This is stupidity, because the argument was that the Black man wanted to wed the White woman.

The Court decided on neutrality because it did not matter if the Black wanted to wed the White, or the White wanted to wed the Black. This is almost laughable if not for the Loving v. Virginia case in 1967. Today, we have people wanting to wed "illegals" to make them legal. The Court had found a creative way to deal with this also.

I'll bet many of you did not know about the civil rights case of 1883. In 1875, the Civil Rights Act was struck down by the courts. Later in 1883, we see five separate challenges to the 1875 act. Here, if the courts would have upheld the 1875 Civil Rights Bill, they would have altered this kind of racism in a huge way.

The Court was not having this, just like the Court is not having any "illegals" today. Bring them to the Court if you want. We, the Court, will order deportation.

Plessy v. Ferguson (1899): This case is known to many of you, or it should be. Perhaps you remember the old separate-but-equal phrase? The Supreme Court gave in to racist people and the racist political pressure of the time. The Court rule manipulated the 14th Amendment by finding a way to keep public institutions separated. Scary here. Today, "illegals" are afraid to use some public accommodations for fear of being discovered and deported.

Immigration laws, racism and the courts continued

with my apple juice in hand, let's get started. I want to hit you hard with more racist Supreme Court cases.

Cumming v. Richmond (1899): In this case we had three Black families moved to act because of the closing of the community's only public Black high school.

All the families wanted were for their children to complete their school year at the White high school.

Why the White school? If I have to answer this by now, you are lost. Let me throw you this to assist: It took the Court a short time to conclude that if there were no suitable schools in a given district (think of a poor school in your district), and then Black students would simply have to do without an education.

Today, I ask you this: In the "illegal immigrant" debate or the argument against "illegals," how many times you have heard it said that they will overburden our schools? The KKK said it better when influencing the Court. The KKK promoted the idea that "niggers," like our "illegals," would mix with their White female girls in schools. This scared the s$$@ out of them.

Ozawa v. United States (1922): Time to start on the Japanese. No one is left out — no one of color, that is.

Here comes Tako Ozawa attempting to fulfill his dream of acculturation and assimilation; he tried to become a United States citizen. Curious — at that time this luxury was limited to Whites and African Americans. Osawa would put a different spin on the argument. No doubt Ozawa knew that using race in a court having a history of supporting the race-based construct would instead challenge the constitutionality of the law.

Being taught that White was power, Ozawa argued that Japanese Americans were White. One can see the justices in the backrooms cracking Japanese features jokes before returning in black robes rejecting this argument. Ozawa lost his case.

Remember one thing as you read any case presented previously and hereafter: The president appoints the Supreme Court justices, all of whom are confirmed by Congress. Take a moment and match the dates of these decisions with the presidents of the time. One may find that that president owned slaves or had Black servants, as did many in Congress.

I just got this idea. You do the research. See how correct this assertion may prove.

United States v. Thind (1923): I warned you that no one and no race are left out of the United States Supreme Court's vitriol. Bhagat Singh, not only an Indian-American but an Army veteran as well, willing to give his life so that the justices would have the freedom to make racist decisions, attempted the same argument as Osawa. In my humble opinion here, he no doubt thought being an Army veteran would have some influence.

Because of my presentation thus far, is there any need to tell you that the justices rejected this argument, concluding that Indians, too, are not White? Hang on just one minute. What if "illegals" used this same argument today to gain access in the United States? All "illegals" should burden the Court with this we-are-White argument. Everyone remember that if this happens it was my idea.

Lam v. Rice (1927): Another race of people come before the Court. Any of you remember or know about the Oriental Exclusion Act of 1924, passed by Congress? You know I was going to bring Congress into this mess. It was my desire to wait for a more propitious moment; however, it's just too tempting to do it now, now that I am on this chronological thing, which I shall shift from later.

The purpose of the act was to reduce the immigration from Asia. I repeat: reduce immigration from Asia. This one is complicated. Having four degrees, one being a paralegal degree, while working on my Master's (a cheap plug about myself), let me explain as simply as possible.

The Court had to be creative here, because being born in the United Sates made the Lams citizens. Their nine-year-old daughter Martha Lum (they gave her an American name for reasons you can well imagine) lived in Mississippi. Their daughter had to attend school, however, and during this time Mississippi had racially segregated schools.

The Lams wanted their daughter to attend a well-organized, wealthy White school. No, no, no, the Court said. The Court didn't use those exact words, but that was the effect of their decision. However, this is what happened.

Hirabayashi v. United States (1943): Anyone remember World War II from your high school civics classes? President Roosevelt issued an executive order holding down the rights of Japanese Americans. You have to remember this one: It was said that 110,000 (likely more) Japanese would be moved to internment camps.

One brave man named Hirabayashi would challenge the executive order. He won. Ha, got you. Of course he didn't — the U.S. Supreme Court told him and his people to get their butts to the camps.

I have made some strong claims with respect to racism, the Court, politics and immigration. More importantly, these claims have been supported by Findings of Fact, Conclusion of Law, and Order of the Supreme Court. You shall see this phrase used throughout my claims and supporting facts.

Take a break, but do return — you have only read my preamble.

Immigration law: control, yes, but justice too

Our brightest and darkest moments in history have their foundation in our courts. Getting back to my previous claims that immigration law has a direct causal relationship to racism, this type of racism is inextricably connected to our United States court system. My claims to this have been supported by actual court cases pointed out in my previous columns and supporting evidence on this matter.

It's time to shift a little, allowing me to bring in other forces that assist in this immigration debate. It's difficult to avoid factors such as economic and educational factors that have direct connections to the movement of immigration law, which sustains itself over periods of time.

It's remarkable that with economic and education factors, outdated immigration law sustains itself because this evolution remains protected in a system of plutocracy. Simply, this allows the minority, the folks with the money, to control politics and have things go as they see fit.

You must understand my view. The foundation of immigration law, its root, the concrete it stands on is so strong that immigration law is almost untouchable because plutocracy influences politics. Thus, the political system, no matter how much we are taught about democracy, controls anyone that is not a citizen.

More powerfully, its lawmakers (politicians) control what makes one legal, or a citizen. This is a heavy-duty concept. This is a very strong factor when looking at money, law and politics.

The courts share much blame for the hatred associated with the United States and its people and shares in the acceptance of this terrible history of the treatment of people of color, the passing of the Chinese exclusion law, and the legalization of slavery. It should surprise no one that the courts, without delay, passed immigration laws aimed at people of color.

Racist immigration law is exactly what one should reasonably conclude and expect from the history of our courts. Can't you see more clearly this casual relationship between the courts and politicians when it come to immigration laws and race?

You still don't get it? What must I do to get you to understand how easily you accept a person of your own race, yet so easily call a person of another race illegal? Let me sidekick the other side of your brain. Let me educate some of you.

Remember the Chinese Exclusion case? Man, I work with Chinese and Whites who've never heard of this case. This is from the U.S. Supreme Court: "The power of exclusion of foreigners is an incident of sovereignty belonging to the government of the United States, as a part of its sovereign powers delegated by the Constitution."

My claim of the courts and their causal relationship to racism and politics is clear. It's easily seen that the court enforces the Constitution, which was created by politicians who appoint the justices who will enforce the Constitution. My claim is simple, and the evidence speaks loudly for itself. I enjoy lifting weights, so let me throw more weight on my claim herein. In *Fong Yue Ting v. United States*, the court issued this opinion: "The right of a nation to expel or deport foreigners is as absolute and unqualified as the right to prohibit and prevent their entrance into the country."

I like being in the law library arguing facts supported by court conclusions, wording, and findings. I offer anyone to argue against my claims. You cannot, because my facts are irrefutable.

Take this historic racist immigration decision — let me tell the story.

It was 1924, when racism was all through the House. In 1924, the national origins quota deal was passed. A lawmaker must have proudly stood on the floor and said, "These doggone non-citizens must never become citizens. We need our friends on the other side to join us in passing this law that will forever and for the sake of our children and the awful prospect of race-mixing — hell, let me cut the chase. I'm preaching to the choir. Let's vote and pass this thing and keep those Asians who think they are White like us from naturalizing."

Yawl knows that's how it was said. I was not on location in 1924, but heck, bet I got it right.

If you missed my last two columns on this subject, you are lost. My plan is to submit this final prospectus to every, yes, every member in Congress. While we must have some control with respect to immigration law, the issue of justice for all must be served.

A white supremacist group rallied against illegal immigration in Los Angeles city centre on April 18, 2010 as hundreds of counter-protesters gathered in a tense standoff that resulted several arrests, thrown rocks and police in riot gear.

Police officers stood between the white supremacists and counter-demonstrators on the south lawn of Los Angeles' City Hall, where about 50 members of the National Socialist Movement waved American flags and swastika banners for about an hour.

The white supremacists, many of them wearing flack helmets and black military fatigue uniforms, shouted 'Sieg Heil' before each of their speakers took the podium to taunt counter-protesters with racial, anti-Semitic and misogynistic epithets.

I want to bring your attention back to my Preamble regarding the KKK rally in Los Angeles because people get caught up in the denial game of that was in the past. The sagacity presented in my argument is having the intelligence to throw the present at you in my direct intent to have you, the reader, come back to the reality of today, in terms of your thought process having its roots in the historical past of racism and immigration laws in today's society.

Previously I mentioned the hate of Asians easily seen in exclusion laws. The question and issue is whether by nationalizing hate laws, does this assist one in seeing oneself as patriotic, thus, making it easier, or perhaps normal to hate because the law justifies such hate, therefore, allowing some kind of release from shame and guilt because the highest court says it acceptable? This is why; one must be forced to think as an individual in hopes of undoing racism and unfairness with respect to immigration laws.

Considering the above-paragraph re-read the previous cases cited herein, before moving on to the next paragraph.

This is worth repeating: The question and issue is whether by nationalizing hate laws, does this assist one in seeing oneself as patriotic, thus, making it easier, or perhaps normal to hate because the law justifies such hate, therefore, allowing some kind of release from shame and guilt because the highest court says it acceptable?

Cutting the chase, let me provide you with further court decisions without the courts long lengthy arguments because the arguments as not as important as the court's rulings. The reality is that the Justices were so full of hate the Plaintiff's argument was a waste of time anyways.

In Unites Sates v. Thind, the court held that an immigrant from India (yes, they were targets to) was not White and therefore was ineligible for naturalization. Let me interject. What is amazing is the similarity in some of these cases in terms of rulings. An example: In Ozawa v. United States, the courts held that a Japanese immigrant, as a non-White, could not naturalize. When looking at the cases provided herein, you must hear a voice over and over inside that tiny brain, perhaps that racist brain, that racial impasse brain you may have, all constructed from institutional racism to maintain a race based construct, in this case, keeping America White. Let me stop and go on. Sorry. The court's willful, intentional, and wrongful and in my opinion unlawful manipulation of the rights of people of color is as much alive today as during the times of Dread Scott v. Sanford in which those people on the bench held that a freed Blackman was not a citizen. In my opinion all of the cases mentioned herein, was for adding racial strength reaching all over this country carried out by the federal courts.

I assert with irrefutable evidence as presented by the courts that racism, yes, despite having a Black president, shall continue to influence the immigration debate and the exclusion of innocent people. Yes, let's exclude all people that would cause us harm, those that want to destroy our people, our country. However, we cannot let racism, using the fear of skin color, be the most unmentioned deciding factors. We have been conditioned to do so.

The 13-14th Amendments are considered the Civil War Amendments. Anyone learned in law is aware of these Amendments. Others should know unless you skipped your high school's Civics class. After many were killed fighting in the Civil War, Congress would still pass a pool of racist immigration laws that had the harshest treatment on people looking like me - African Americans. Knowing this, how, can I call another man/woman looking as I, illegal? How can you call another person looking like yourself illegal so easily?

When the highest court in the land makes rulings as provided herein, this makes immigration law and prohibition socially acceptable and legally justified. Seeing the relationship between government (politics) and the courts, Congress had many so-called debates which were designed to pit one racial group against another. In such floor debates members of Congress would conclude that Chinese folks could be treated more shit$# than Blacks (some used "N") because the Chinese are foreigners and the Negro is native. On your own study linguistics racism and see the power of words that I have used.

Racism, Immigration, claims and irrefutable evidence

If you haven't noticed, let me tell you what I have so clearly been doing with this Immigration, race and government thing. I have used the rulings of the court, which are irrefutable because the rulings did occur. This with my wisdom to add credibility to my opinions, thereby, making it hard for you to disagree that immigration law, perhaps your attitude towards immigrants, the non-threatening immigrant, have been carefully designed. This has to be a cathartic moment for you to realize this at this time in your life. A few of you still needing some undoing racism therapy let me continue.

What about the quota word? You have been tricked into believing that the word quota has to do with hiring of Blacks and women. As only I, the one with untouchable wisdom can do, shall provide you with the truth. It was 1924 (hear my voice saying this with a touch of poetry) our fellow Congressman, having the desire to protect Whiteness, created the Q, word being Quota. Let me stop being silly. Our, no, your Congressman, no doubt influenced by previous court rulings and racist constituents, would become inventors of a system that would promote stability in the ethnic make- up of our great country. Now, as recent as 1924, we see the race based construct gain more power because White immigrants were favored arriving from Northern and Western Europe. By the way the prefix "EU" means good. No extra charge. Hold on. Some of you people may be thinking that this Lucky sounds racist. Just telling the truth folks. Let me continue. The courts had to justify the Whites (having made previous conclusions about people of color and immigration) by using a testing tool. Keep in mind because of hate, discrimination in public accommodations, no way could people of color meet the following; all aliens over sixteen years of age, capable of reading, but could not read English language, or some other language (not Ebonics yawl) language or dialect, they covered it all yawl, to include Hebrew and Yiddish (did I spell Yiddish correctly?) Let me stop clowning. The point being in theory, the test purpose was to restrict immigration of non-English speakers, oh, oh, including Italians, Russians, Poles, Hungarians, Greeks, Asians and no doubt, I missed a few. Add the ones I missed yourself. Likely, you'll be right.

Let me cut the bullshit. In 1924 the "Q" word was used to keep America White, long before it was used in the workplace. All of the sudden it became a bad word after the Title VII Civil Rights Act. What else did this accomplish? White/European power. The Ku Klux Klan philosophy of keeping the superior race. Make no mistake. The KKK yesterday, today, very much influence today's politicians and immigration law. Prove me wrong.

The racist "Q" system was designed to prevent Asians, Africans and other non-Whites from entering the United States. I believe the main focus was on Africa. I don't have the statistics, but I'll bet Snickers that in comparison, less immigration comes from Africa. I say this as a statement, not a question.

This "Q" system was later weakened. The 1965 Act did away with the national origins clause, but slickly placed a 20 thousand limit on immigrants from some nations. However, immigration laws today, yes, with a Black president, continue to favor Whites. One does not have to look far to witness a disparately unfavorable outcome on non-citizens of color.

Where are we today? Let me tell you what I think about the Immigration Act of 1990. While the Act attempted to focus on concerns of race, once again some of you were fooled. But not with my superior wisdom. Out with the "Q" word. We, the members of Congress would like to introduce a kinder phrase. The Immigrant Visa Program. Which group of people benefited. The Irish. 1990s, during this visa program, Whites benefited. This program was designed for White immigrants.

Conclusion on Immigration Law and Racism

Remember. I asked the question about people from Poland coming to the United States blending in on construction jobs with no problem. This is why? The visa program offered 40% of visas are given to Irish Immigrants. This, with the fact that records indicate that in 1995, the leading favored getting such visas were people from Poland. This is Welfare, preference and double standards. This alone ought to make any person of color furious. And you have the audacity to call a person that looks like you, the color as yourself, illegal. You had better think twice before doing so again. One race gives and takes from another. This is evil and wrong.

Today's immigration laws are racist with irrefutable disparate impact on any person of color, their children and families. Whites are left out of the equation when it comes to conversation, debate about immigration. It always has to do with people of color.

We see law enforcement, government, the courts, the KKK and other hate groups, all with a say in this immigration thing. I ask you to think White when you talk about immigration laws because you will already by condition think colored people.

What do you say to people that have left their country because of civil war, political and religious persecution, including genocide. We allow Whites easy access. But not people of color. What about the Jews that support immigration laws today? Have the Jews forgotten Roosevelt. The Jews must have cried out, Roosevelt, why, has thou forsaken us? Roosevelt turned his back on the Jews running from Hitler. Today, Jews support immigration laws preventing humans from trying to get away from persecution and genocide.

Congress can honor visa laws favoring White immigrants. But when it comes to people fleeing Haiti we witness racist policies. One does not have to guess the reasons that Haitians, yes, under President Clinton, were the new targets of racist immigration laws having our Armed forces pluck them form the seas, holding them in the sun for days, for no other compelling argument than race.

Today, politicians are elected with tough talk on immigration laws. Never, about Whites, but restricting the movement on people of color. Sadly. People of color feeling the need to assimilate, to fit in, to be White, buy into the hype.

I am asking you to find room for a new debate. New, judicial review on this matter of immigration with race as it ugly foundation. How, can immigration law be justified if it is injustice? It cannot be justice, if applied because of race and not because of a country of real threat. Plutocracy, plenary power, and racism all have influence in our courts, or legislative and judicial branch of government as clearly shown in my writings. To undo this, to create the justice of balance, starts with you, the individual. Immigration law must be brought into the public law, public focus with awareness of injustice. Immigration law must be applied, not separated from our Constitution. If we continue to walk down this trap, we shall get caught in it ourselves.

To seal our boarders from real threat is to be done without question. But to seal it because of race alone is evil and destroys our Constitution. The United States must reach a new level of law. The icons of immigration of justice. It was Truman that admitted that the quota system was founded on the concept that people with American or Irish names were better than others including Greek, Polish and Jews. Yet, these same subjugated classes easily support laws preventing the movement of their own people. One must ask himself or herself why?

The term immigration, when used with immigration law, has a terrifying outcome. Immigration law oppresses, subjugates, and reinforces this pseudo adaptation of inferiority in its targets, while providing a sense of superiority to the perpetrators. This is the foundation of racism. This is the 21st century approach towards domestic subordination, despite a Black president. Preventing movement for no other reason but race is the enemy of diversity. Exclusion is exclusion. One cannot mention exclusion without the inevitable expectation of this what I call) mosaic augmentation of injustice, inequality, racism, power and discrimination.

If you are a person of color, I am directing you to think twice before calling a human that looks like you illegal. If you are White, you must challenge your thought process by recognizing double standards and preference given to White immigrants when deciding your new position with respect to Immigration Law and racism.

God bless not only America, but its people because in Heaven, there will be no boarders to cross.

Lucky Rosenbloom welcomes reader responses to 612-661-0923, or email him at l.rosenbloom@yahoo.com

Opinion 39

Lies my teacher told me about Democrats

Brother Lucky is not surprised by the responses received about the real Democrats relevant to their history and treatment of Black people. Many of you during elementary and secondary school and through college have been told of the goodness of liberal Democrats. This has been their way of redemption and projection: redemption through social programs that have crippled Black mothers and projection by throwing their characteristics of hate on Republicans.

Thomas "Daddy" Rice was one of our friendly White Southern Democrats that gave birth to the Jim Crow laws in 1828. However, friendly "Daddy" could not have done this without the support of other Southern Democrats wanting to keep Blacks in their place. Thus, these supporting Democrats would become "Daddy's" encouragement, giving birth to Blacks having to tip their hats and step aside as Whites would approach. Now, explain the reasons for our never being told this about Democrats in school?

Our history teachers should have instructed. By 1880s, Jim Crow had become legal and justified racial laws, created a race-based society and racial customs in the South that protected White Democrats' social legal, economics and political domination of Blacks. "My students," my teacher should have said, "there is more: White Southern Democrats moved to segregate Blacks using Blacks and White drinking fountains; and Lucky, do you know these people deprived you of your right to vote?"

The teacher should have turned to another student and said, "Tracy, White Democrats in the south subjected your grandmother to verbal abuse and rape." The teacher should have said, "I want my class to know that these Southern Democrats subjected your relatives to violence, discrimination and hangings without redress to the courts all with support of White liberal Democrats."

Many of my readers have come to understand we have been lied to not only by our teachers but also local Black historians. Local Black leaders and historians are surprised by the growing number of young people attacking not being taught the truth about White Democrats and are further surprised by the number of young Blacks looking at Republicans and / or other political affiliates.

Lies my teacher told me about Democrats being my protection from racist Republicans projected hate onto people who didn't have much do with slavery. Our teachers should have told us that because of White Southern slave owners, who were Democrats, and later because of Jim Crow, many of your ancestors were sold into slavery and lynched, women were raped, children were killed, and no records were maintained of their births.

"Well, my class of sixth graders, this could be hard to accept, but because of all of this at the hands of White Southern Democrats, freedmen and freedwomen attempted to rebuild families horrified by slavery. It gets worse, my students. Because of Democrats in the South, tens of thousands of children – as gorgeous as all of you in my class were, well, oh, the Democrats who sold your parents, brothers, sisters, and your big mamma are to other Southern White Democrats."

"However, after slavery, my students, Blacks - being the strong people that you are, not weak and needing handouts – would place ads in newspapers looking for their relatives. My students, I could get in trouble for doing this, but I would like to read one such advertisement White liberals in our schools are hiding: "Sam, I dove wishes to know the whereabouts of his mother Areno, his sisters Maria, Neziah, and Peggy and his brother Edmund sold in Richmond. There's a $200 reward for our daughter Polly and our son, who George Washington carried away as slaves. Next week, if I am not fired, I will teach you the truth as to why the names in these types of letters were not African names. Hope to see all of you next week."

I am the columnist bringing you the truth. Over the years, I have watched Black Democrats criticize me by calling me the only Black Republican, and attempt to discredit me in the community, the governor's office and in the state legislature. I have outlasted all attempts because of my intelligence, honesty, integrity and superior endurance with the support of many of you, the open-minded reader.

Lucky does not vacillate. My word is my word. When I state my position, leadership is demonstrated because people know my steadiness, leaving guessing out of the equation. Simply, I am right. This is the reason no one will debate me face to face, but would rather write responses in some other form. So, once again, Lucky Rosenbloom has spoken. Follow the leader columnist.

Lucky Rosenbloom welcomes reader responses to 612-661-0923, or email him at l.rosenbloom@yahoo.com

Opinion 40

Big, bad and talking about a dead man

Tiger Jack Rosenbloom, my father, worked out of a little shack on a corner of St. Paul's Dale Street for half a century, selling candy to the kids and firewood to adults, waving to the passing cars and putting a familiar face on Rondo. He became an emblem of a largely Black part of the city that was mostly unknown to Whites.

Tiger Jack, a boxer in his youth, died three years ago at age 94, having outlived Rondo (which was bulldozed for construction of Interstate Hwy. 94) and most of his contemporaries. Okay, sad for the neighborhood and for his family. Check. Don't you love the implication that Whites are expected to know every neighborhood in the cities, but that it's especially bad if they don't know the "largely Black" parts?

After he died, his shack went on exhibit at the Minnesota Historical Society, along with a cardboard cutout of the man who came to personify St. Paul's Black community. But that's the problem; and no, it's not really the problem that a cardboard cutout is really damn tacky...

The image of Rondo he left was a cardboard cutout, a superficial and stereotyped representation of a complex community. With Rondo Days being celebrated this weekend – and with no disrespect to Tiger Jack's memory intended – I asked three Black community leaders (all of whom knew Tiger Jack) to talk about the man and the meaning of his image.

I'm calling bullsh*t on the "no disrespect" line, as you'll soon see. But first, Leader #1: "Tiger Jack makes the White community comfortable," says Mahmoud El-Kati, a longtime professor of African-American history on leave from Macalester College in St. Paul. Although Tiger Jack was a "wonderful guy", says El-Kati, the image he left "is not a complex image; he's not stirring up anything or agitating or anything like that. He's not raising hell, as you could say about just about anyone else in those days. The Twin Cities has a very rich civil rights history, but if you're talking about the struggle, his name doesn't come up."

So everybody out there with dark skin, if you make people comfortable, aren't stirring up or agitating or raising hell, you aren't part of "the struggle", and therefore…what? You're not "complex" enough? You're a traitor to your "race"? What?

"No disrespect" indeed.

"The White community is very good at celebrating Black individuals", says El-Kati, 67. He further commented, "Especially if they are an athlete or an entertainer." The individual becomes bigger than the life of the community itself, but the individual is one-dimensional. The community is complex, but it's almost like it's not even there to many Whites."

Well there's where we differ, Mr. El-Kati: I don't give a rat's furry, diseased hindquarters about any "community". Communities are defined by individuals, not the other way around. Someone who identifies him/herself as part of a "community" ahead of being a human being like everyone around them is falling victim to the idea that a person's environment defines everything about them, an idea I flatly reject.

Time for Leader #2: William Finney, St. Paul's recently retired police chief, grew up on Rondo Avenue. He said, "The problem with Tiger Jack's fame is that it has obscured the achievements of Black professionals who were Rondo's real role models, but whose names are unknown outside the community." "Rondo produced doctors, pharmacists, undertakers and cops", Finney says. Yet, it was Tiger Jack who came to symbolize Rondo.

A community member said, "I first heard of Tiger Jack when he died, but every year when Rondo Days comes around I hear about the neighborhood and how said it was that it was flattened." "Tiger Jack always appeared subservient to people he thought were powerful," says Finney. "It was like he was on stage, or in a show. We were raised in the '60s and didn't like that. He was an anachronism…He was all the stuff we didn't want to be and that we wanted to go away."

He was also 40 years older than you, Mr. Finney, and from a very different generation. During the '60s he was already in/near his own 60s, an age at which most people seem to want peace and quiet.

Lucky Rosenbloom welcomes reader responses to 612-661-0923, or email him at l.rosenbloom@yahoo.com

Opinion 41

Black folks can't blame Bush anymore

Here I am, sitting in my music room surrounded by drum machines, electronic keyboards, high-powered amps, music sheets and stuff like that – you know musician stuff. I must write a tune with a good hook to celebrate Obama's presidency. Should the movement be in 2/4, 3/4, 5/4 or 4/4?

The tempo is also integral to capturing one's attention. Can't be too fast, can't be too slow. I'll need a hook that people can catch on to. Let me go with the regular 4/4 for soul. My hook: "Can't blame Bush anymore."

I am ready for the lyrics. Don't forget the hook, "Can't blame Bush anymore." Do you remember attending meetings within local Black organizations and hearing leaders blame Bush for them not being able to do anything to move the Black community forward? Hit it – "Can't blame Bush anymore."

I remember listening to a group of students, some high on drugs, reporting to school late blaming Bush for not having enough credits to graduate and acting as though they had no reason to try because life seemed useless under the Bush administration. Hit it – "Can't blame Bush anymore."

Come on now. Think a moment for yourselves. Think of all the people, all the meetings you've attended over the years and heard people blame Bush for their setbacks and / or for others setbacks. Hit it – "Can't blame Bush anymore."

So tell me, as Black leaders and members of Black organization continue to fail our community, who are you going to blame? Hit it – "Can't blame Bush anymore."

You heard it here first. Liberals by the end of summer 2009 will place blame on Obama as they did Bush. You see, Obama promotes self-reliance. Obama is the antithesis of everything molded around group failure, group victims, preferences, entitlements, and dependency programs that some Black leaders continue to advocate.

As Obama moves closer to the center, as Obama makes good on his comment to end programs that do not work, Black liberals having membership in agencies failing our communities will be the target of Obama's shut-them-down movement.

I said it here first. The new blame will shift to Obama because – hit it – "Can't blame Bush anymore."

I believe that Obama is going to be in battle with the Affirmative Action liberal Blacks, such as Jackson. Remember the microphone incident? Let me continue. Obama is going to be in battle with people like Jackson and

Sharpton because Obama understands that repentance liberalism is the second White Southern Democrat betrayal of Black people leading to oppression and Black delusion.

Readers, it becomes very simple. From this reality, Blacks hit it – "Can't blame Bush anymore." They will remain quiet, or shift blame towards Obama for their inability to reorganize their dependency on government programs back into focus.

I believe that Obama will continue to move Black beyond welfare and handouts because he knows that both welfare and Affirmative Action robs people of full responsibility and respect which promotes inner inferiority. Blacks blaming Bush for an end to such programs that really started with Clinton are now at a loss with Obama. They now will not be able to blame Bush.

It will be worth watching to see the shift of blame as Blacks become more aware of the Obama dichotomy. Hit it – "Can't blame Bush anymore."

Let's talk about taxes. We never could blame Bush for this one because Republicans are about holding down taxes. However, let us look at Obama's tax plan, which means nothing as local Democrats raise property and other taxes to support big spending. Almost forgot my hook; hit it – "Can't blame Bush anymore."

Under Obama if you earn less than 19k, one should save $567. At 19k-39k, there is about $892 in savings. At 66k-111k, here is the problem. With the savings, you'll never see the money. Well, you will see the savings long enough to pay out the local raised taxes by your favorite Democrats.

When this happens, hit it – "Can't blame Bush anymore." I'll stop my song for now. However, not to worry, more lyrics shall come soon.

Council on Black Minnesotans

Attending a meeting at the CBM, a group of Black youth presented their idea for wanting to have a primary-seatbelt law in Minnesota. The youth's research shows that such a law would lower the number of Blacks being killed in car accidents in urban America.

After the youth left some indicated the law would be used for racial profiling, allowing police to pull Black youth over discovering drugs in their cars. This is the most stupid argument yet. The police have more reasons to pull a person over without the primary-seatbelt law. Furthermore, Black youth should not be driving while smoking weed, drinking, or with weapons in their cars anyway.

Rosenbloom welcomes reader responses to 612-661-0923, l.rosenbloom@yahoo.com

Opinion 42

Conservatives enjoy lower blood pressure

We do not have to travel far to experience hate. We have it right in our backyard. Housing, jobs, economics, starting businesses, obtaining home loans – one could go on and on.

Our communities are controlled by Democrats in the city council, at the state level, and all the way to Washington. All these loving Democrats, please, anyone, tell me how we can have so much discrimination in our communities? All the love Democrats have for us...Well, let me get to my point.

Discrimination causes health problems. Can you imagine the stress, the pain that we have to deal with daily? From the moment we leave our homes, the scrutiny is on in stores, applying for jobs, going to work wondering when some hate-filled devil will harass you, being turned down for a loan, having to have and show more for housing, and looking behind yourself hoping not to be pulled over by law enforcement.

I am not talking about in some distant area but right here in an area surrounded by loving Democrats who will not or cannot do anything about any of it to any meaningful outcomes. Racial discrimination, no doubt causes high blood pressure in Blacks, and Democrats historically have been the source of discrimination. Think about your parents and grandparents who have died from high blood pressure. All of their lives at work or wherever, they have had to deal with discrimination in our own communities under the control of Democrats for over 50 years.

Once internalized, discrimination creates a high risk for high blood pressure. This is a factor Black health professionals must consider with high blood pressure diagnoses. Lawyers must consider this in Title VII civil rights suits when their clients suddenly experience high blood pressure as a direct result of dealing with discrimination.

Try to understand my point. I am not a medical professional. However, I'd like to believe my ability to reason, analyze, build from current knowledge and offer substantive conclusions are acceptable to humans having reasonable prudence.

It's been said that Blacks get hypertension one-third more often than Whites. We have learned that Blacks get it earlier in life and suffer more severe health problems. Perhaps this is Lucky logic, but don't we experience racism as early as elementary school through high school and into adulthood?

Why it is that working-class Blacks are more likely to have high blood pressure than professionals? Let me tell you the answer: The physical demands associated with the daily racism, must amount to great physiological effect and psychological stress causing health problems over the years. Really, Black health professionals must seriously look at my point.

My father, Tiger Jack, operated his own business for over 57 years and died of natural causes at age 93. On the other hand, my mother worked a job for over 37 years dealing with racism and developed high blood pressure. Democrats must look at discrimination as similar to high salt intake and other factors as a cause of high blood pressure. Black women in the working class, such as my mother, have higher blood pressure because women in our society internalize racism more, because they are bullied into remaining quiet and accepting racism as some kind of inevitability.

I offer this for debate: Black conservatives, regardless of gender, who refuse to accept racism and offer a challenge when confronted with racism from the liberals, have the lowest incidents of high blood pressure.

Lucky Rosenbloom welcomes reader responses to 612-661-0923, or email him at l.rosenbloom@yahoo.com

Opinion 43

Democrats: Sex, players and holla, holla!

When it to come to teaching people about sex in today's society, I am going to use the Democrats as examples of truth, justice and the American way. I'm going to tell folks that when it comes to sex, I hate to admit it but Democrats have got the Republicans licked. So, let's talk about sex, players and holla, holla!

It was Sen. Ted Kennedy that would testify in defense of his nephew accused of rape, using his family history to influence the jury in 1991. So, before you rape an innocent member of society, you must make sure that you have family influence. If not, don't do the crime, if you can't do the time. Say it with me; Holla, holla!

Let's talk about sex. Former Rep. Mel Reynolds, the Illinois Democrat, was convicted of 12 counts of sexual assault with a 16-year-old. President Bill Clinton pardoned him before leaving office. Makes you wonder if Clinton gave him a cigar up on his release? Say it with me, holla, holla!

Rep. Gerry Studds, living up to his stud image, was censured for a sexual relationship with an underage male page in 1983. Being the Democrat icon of a stud, he was returned to office for six more terms. Say it with me, holla, holla!

Rep. Wayne Hays: This Democrat hired an unqualified secretary for sexual acts. Does this make you wonder the types of Sen. Brock Adams:

This Democrat was doing some serious pimpin'without the "g" on the end? The other Democrats were hatin' (not hating, because this is too proper for Democrat players) because he was forced to stop his run for office after allegations of drugging, assault and rape.

You see he failed the main criteria; getting elected for protection. Say it with me. The player's player dogged Adams. Say it with me, holla, holla!

Rep. Barney Frank: This Democrat player hired a male prostitute who ran a prostitution service from the player's (Frank's) residence in the 1980s. Say it with me, holla, holla!

I'm telling you, it's hard keeping up with these Democrat players, but this columnist is on his game. Holla, holla! Let me continue.

Rep. Gus Savage, being the savage of the Democrat players club, although he and Bill would battle for this recognition, was accused of playing piano (my nice way of saying fondling a Peace Corp Volunteer) in 1989 while on a trip to Africa. The House Ethics Committee working under the auspices of the Democrat Players Club decided against disciplinary action in 1990. Say it with me, holla, holla!

Sen. Daniel Inouye, hip hop for "I know you say yes" (come on give me a holla, holla, for the creativity on his name), was accused in the 1990s by several women of sexual harassment. Here, the Democrats Players club would drop an investigation on this 82-year-old senator. Say it with me, holla, holla!

So, let us develop our own code words when saying hello to any elected official that is a Democrat. Upon shaking his hand – I did not say her – say, when it comes to sex, truth, players and the American way, we Democrats perform better than Republicans, using the trademark closing: Say it with me, holla, holla!

Lucky Rosenbloom welcomes reader responses to 612-661-0923, l.rosenbloom@yahoo.com

Opinion 44

The evil Democrat doctor

J. Marion Sims, believed to be the father of gynecology and known Democrat, won distinction by improving the speculum and developing a surgical technique to correct abnormalities between the vagina and the bladder. Dr. Sims procedure was tried on White women only after he had experienced with it repeatedly on slave women without their consent and without anesthesia. – A quote from a famous Democrat

Americans, at our best, value the life we see in one another and must always

remember that even the unwanted have worth. And our country must abandon all the habits of racism because we cannot carry the message of freedom and the baggage of bigotry at the same time.

Many of you accept this quote with meaning, value and with socially applicable worthiness. Now, forgive my ensnaring behavior. Read the quote again with the reality that President Bush said it. Does it have the same powerful meaning?

Stop being a hater.

I really don't give a rat's dead small about Democrats and liberals' vitriol and/or attempting to cause me problems in the community because of my recent columns, "Lies my teachers told me about Democrats." I have come to understand with acuity this "shame game" of Democrats acting out in the community, when a refusing-to-be-a-victim strong Black person such as me, steps offs the plantation of group dependency to individual responsibility and self-reliance.

For the many of you that call, email, or talk with me in public and have reached a cathartic reality that Democrats are not our Gods, for those of you that compliment my sagacity and courage with respect to the truths about Democrats, I say your ability to recognize my character as being better when compared to the liberal is excellent.

So, liberals continue to turn your heads and act as if you can't stand this conservative columnist. Doing so only provides motivation to continue and believe me, I shall not stand down.

Family ties

Have you heard the news? Al Sharpton, civil rights activist, and Strom Thurmond (if you look up the word segregation, his picture would be next to the definition) have some close connection. Rev. Al's ancestors were slaves owned by relatives of Strom. I found a picture of Strom, and held it next to one of Al. Wow! These two really look similar in facial features right down to their hair. Find a picture of these two, and hold them next to each other. I am telling you, you'll see the resemblance.

Minnesota Department of Commerce investigates

This columnist conducted research into Countrywide Home Loans because of their practices in a court case filed in Hennepin County (number 27-CV-07-2627). The lawyers for Countrywide threatened to obtain a court order to silence some of my findings. This columnist was on to something.

Readers knowing this columnist are aware that it's not easy to scare me with legal threats. I am fully aware of my First Amendment rights. Nevertheless, because of this legal threat, which never materialized after my memorandum to the court (contact me for a copy), this columnist knew he was on to something.

I discovered that Countrywide recently agreed to pay $3.2 million to settle charges brought by the New York State Attorney General Elliot Spitzer because of their racist practices with Black and Latino customers. On July 6, 2007, this columnist hand delivered a letter to the Minnesota Department of Commerce and the Minnesota Attorney General's Office asking for an investigation into Countrywide's practices in Black and Latino communities in Minnesota.

Copies of my findings were also delivered to Gov. Tim Pawlenty, Velma Korbel of the State Human Rights Department and to Michael Jordan of the Human Rights Commission of Minneapolis with a notice of the aforementioned Hennepin County case, which involves a Black man. This case has some similarities to the findings out in New York, in which the judge ordered Countrywide's lawyer to remain in his court and settle the matter. Yes, the court would not let anyone leave until the matter was settled in favor of the brother.

The Minnesota Department of Commerce contacted this columnist and advised that they are now looking into my investigation request. I have not heard from the Minnesota Attorney General's Office, not to mention the AG office's top dog who is a Democrat and the Minnesota Department of Commerce's top dog who is a Republican. This columnist will maintain pressure on the AG office to investigate.

Question: Do you believe that Countrywide's racist practice was isolated to New York? This columnist does not believe their practice was limited to New York. If you have done business with Countrywide and feel as though you were treated unfairly because of race, this columnist would like to know about your experience.

As always, this columnist continues his dedication towards protecting our people and community members.

Lucky Rosenbloom welcomes reader responses to 612-661-0923, or email him at l.rosenbloom@yahoo.com

Opinion 45

Liberal media selects Black leaders

I have never been one to withhold comments regarding the liberal media, so no point in starting today. The liberal media has a malevolent habit of telling White America those people that they feel are worthy to speak for all Black folks in this great country.

From King and Jackson to Sharpton, the media offers leaders that fit into the agency of dependency as opposed to Black leaders who would promote self-reliance. Absent these leaders conditioning Blacks to dependency on government, these people were / are great leaders.

Now, White people are in need of great leadership throughout America. I am going to appoint David Duke / Pastor Ted Haggard as their leader. David Duke / Pastor Ted Haggard offers America's progressive agenda with popular recognition in perilous times guiding White America, being a single voice for all White America.

One can read the liberal media headline now: David Duke / Pastor Ted Haggard (the leader for Whites in America) said, "That our rights are slowly ticking away because Hispanics are taking jobs that no other American would desire. We must stand strong and start applying for such jobs in order that we may hold firm on our traditions and values."

In perilous times, I offer David Duke / Pastor Ted Haggard as your leader, White America. If I could only get every Black media source to portray David Duke / Pastor Ted Haggard as the leader for all White people. Whites would accept the Black media voice as representing their entire culture in reciprocity for Blacks accepting this direction from the liberal White media.

Did anyone get my point here? A friend of mine suggested that I should check with the White people before appointing David Duke / Pastor Ted Haggard as their leader. Wow! The triumph of catharsis. Perhaps Whites ought to give us the same respect by checking with Blacks.

Democrats and the poor

Rep. Keith Ellison must bring realistic ideas to liberals in Washington. Stop those idiots from thinking the poor will be better off by passing laws that will tax the rich.

You see, Keith, the Democrats solution to helping the poor is attacking the rich. The problem is that we can impose higher taxes on the rich; however, this will do nothing for the poor. The rich will remain rich and the poor will only get poorer

Spend more time thinking about ways to make the poor rich, instead of making the rich poor. Accomplish this easily by destroying those agencies that promote dependency, entitlements, preferential treatment, double standards, and cultural provisions that foster helplessness. The poor shall then become rich within 10 years throughout America.

The attack on the rich to help the poor is totally myopic. Democrats promoting this concept have the most brilliant minds of the 17th century.

Overtaxing the rich will foster what Blacks have experienced for years – inertia from poverty. Heavy taxes and government regulation on the rich is retaliation and resentment. These approaches will not help the poor. Somebody say Amen!

Crime victims mistreated by police

Having little sympathy for criminals; I expect police to arrest criminals without making excuses. However, I have all the care for victims of crime mistreated by police, because after the pain of being a victim to be treated like dirt by police is morally repugnant.

I'm asking you for an opportunity to write your story. Have you been the victim of a crime and called the police for assistance only to have been treated with disrespect upon their arrival? Have you called the police about a disturbance only to have them not show up, yet when you call 911 a second time you are told police did respond and you know they never showed up?

This would not happen in Minnetonka. Call me with your story, because after the accumulation of so many, I shall write about selected stories in my June 2007 column. This topic will be included at the conclusion of each monthly column until April 2007. Complaints shall be considered for victims of crime only; criminals need not respond.

Respond at 612 661.0923 or email l.rosenbloom@yahoo.com

Opinion 46

Survivor series separates the races

Liberal media promotes stereotypes 21st-century style

How many of you remember this program?

Here is my precis regarding the television program *Survivor* that positions tribe against tribe using racial separation. Now, the White tribe can't be trusted, because when other tribe members come to their rescue, they are likely to capture and enslave the other tribes, while spreading diseases, killing off all but the Black tribe.

Now, the Black tribe because of their ability to withstand heat and superior athleticism could win, if not for the water and not being able to swim, because the sisters ain't getting their hair wet.

The Hispanic tribe will have stamina and a good chance of winning because of the skills they can use from living in the desert and going without food while hiding and waiting to cross the border. The Asian tribe could win because of their above-average intelligence and living in huts and surviving rainstorms; however, computers are not in the jungle.

Due to fairness, which is the network's intent to give the other tribes a chance, the Native Americans were left out because they are ones with the earth. This would have put all the other tribes at an enormous disadvantage.

People of color defend Survivor racism

The above comments are as separating races for this type of competition. This show fostered the stereotypes mentioned, and at the end will entertainment, fun and whatever else one may want to call it will promulgate stereotypes. Maybe, I'll stand corrected. However, unlike others, I have the courage to offer my opinion now, before the end of the series. If this show were produced by Fox (a conservative medium), Blacks would attack its producers. …tasteful; yet, you will likely say nothing to people that talk such as this in your company. Is this not the way hate has developed and racism is sustained because of no one challenging racist stereotypes of others?

One person of color said to me, "Lucky it's just entertainment." I responded, was it not just entertainment when Blacks were lynched as others stood by viewing and laughing? Was it just entertainment when liberal media depicted Blacks with big white eyes, darkened with white teeth and running from their own shadows, while yelling "Yessom, boss"? Another person that defended the show's concept as being fun competition was irresponsive when I mentioned that Hilter himself promulgated superiority under the shield of competition at the Olympic Games.

To both of these individuals, I asked, "So, how will you feel if the White tribe wins, thus proving they have superior survivor skills?" At that point, one wanted to end the conversation, and the other indicated this could be an insult to Dr. King's dream of little Black and White boys and girls walking together holding hands.

A reader responds

Note: Comments from readers have nothing to do with my opinions.

Jennifer White writes: "In my opinion, they (CBS, *Survivor*) are attempting to capitalize on the most loaded issue in America in an effort to perpetuate the stereotypes and misconceptions surrounding race that have been engrained in our society for centuries. They are using the shock value to get ratings and generate dollars, but this is not something new to us. It comes down to the individual on whether or not to support their measures.

"Personally, I will not be tuning in to put more money in the pocket a corporate monster who continues to capitalize at the expense of people of color. I mean, come on, we already know who will win."

Remember the show? *Send your opinions about* Survivor at l.rosenbloom@yahoo.com

Opinion 47

Democrat House Negroes preach gloom and doom

White people don't feel doom when Republicans are in control. Why do Black people feel its doomsday?

Black leaders ought to feel shame, like the oppressor, like they are House Negroes preaching doom in the Black community because Republicans control the House on the national level and both the House and Senate here in Minnesota.

I am going to ask you to think back several columns ago, several years ago, when Lucky Rosenbloom said that one day Republicans would control Minnesota and will have control on the national level. Many said I was crazy, out of my mind, and a few other anti-Luckymania comments.

Once again the Luckster has proven to be ahead of other Black liberal leaders. Simply stated, I am right again. Republicans control the House and Senate in Minnesota and the House in Washington.

Every time the liberal House Negro steps out of the master Democrat house and tells you that your life is over, that you have not a chance to do anything with your life, the Republican is a racist, and anything else this old, tired-out House Negro tells you, you should tell him to go back to that blue-eyed master and let him know that you are a person of self-reliance, that no political party controls your destiny because that destiny belongs to God.

Tell that Democrat House Negro that you shall stand strong, that you will analyze Republican policies such as their message about jobs, reducing government power, making it easier to start your business. Tell that Democrat House Negro that when Republicans reduce government and lower your taxes, then you will be able to keep your home and send your kids to college.

Tell that Democrat House Negro trying to preach doom to the Black family that he is the one who supported Democrats who continue to raise taxes during these hard times. The Democrat is the one who has pushed welfare on our people, developing ghettos and single families living on welfare checks that provide little income, keeping our beautiful Black mothers and children dependent on his system of going nowhere.

Ask that Democrat House Negro how he continues to live high on the hog with his/her expensive car, watches and more while Republicans are in control, yet he tells you that you're doomed under the racist Republican.

Don't you accept this doomsday theory? God loves you. God has a plan for you. You're important to God. Why, this Democrat House Negro comes from the masters' DFL headquarters trying to destroy your spiritual strength. Any Black preaching doom while Republicans are in control is a wicked man.

Can you imagine Malcolm X, King, Vernon Johns teaching you doom, that your life is over because of White Republicans in control? Malcolm would call such preaching wicked and the teachers of such a doomsday message an enemy to Black people.

I'm telling you. The next time one of these Democrat House Negroes tells you your life is in hell because of a Republican, look at his watch, his car, his home. Ask him this question: "If things are so bad, how do you keep so much?"

Let me tell you some things Malcolm X said about White liberals. Malcolm promoted the idea that the White liberal removes your inner desire towards freedom, justice and equality. Malcolm promoted the idea that the White liberal Democrat acts as your friend while telling you what other Whites are doing to harm you.

This is similar to 2010. We have the White liberal, the Democrat House Negro, telling you how God-awful the White Republican is while all along, when the White liberal was in power, our people continued to beg for jobs, justice in the courts, and freedom to send our children to schools of our choice.

Malcolm promoted the idea that Black people must lose all fear of the White man. However, it's the liberal, the Democrat, the Democrat House Negro who now teaches you to fear the White Republican as if he controls your destiny. Do you believe that if Malcolm were with us today, he would be preaching fear of White Republicans?

I am going to follow Republican policies and tell you a different message. I am going to tell you how you can use Republican policies to further your life, to augment your future in positive ways. This is true Black leadership.

We need leaders who can teach you how to grow regardless of whether it's Democrats and/or Republicans in control. Black people have survived slavery, lynchings, and a lot more than Republicans being in control. Don't listen to these Democrat House Negroes trying to keep you loyal. These people are great students of the Willie Lynch theory.

Lucky Rosenbloom welcomes reader responses to l.rosenbloom@yahoo.com. Call my Republican Party policies update line weekly at 612-387-4546.

Opinion 48

To hear more of my opinions call the National Black Political Advisory message line at 612.387.4546. Write P.O. Box 4171 St. Paul, MN 55103

Closing

Wanted: Black leadership during Republican power

We need Black leaders capable of understanding the conservative/Republican ideology. We need Black leaders who have the ability to interpret and apply conservative/Republican policy in immediate, concise and competent ways that benefit Black people.

Many Black leaders lack these proclivities when it comes to Republican policy because of many years of narrow-mindedness and being Uncle Toms to the Democrats. Black leaders have been able to use the arts of persuasion, threats when needed, rewarding as appropriate, and retribution within the Democrat Party.

However, these same arts do not apply within the Republican ranks. Thus, their only option is to promulgate the Republican Party as racist, rich White folks who could care less about Black people.

It's worth studying the above-mentioned because by doing so we can understand the confusion among Black leadership in this time of Republican control on both the national and local levels. I have said it many times in this column and elsewhere: It's dangerous for Blacks to be in one of the major political parties.

By doing so, liberal Black leaders have vilified Republicans to the point that they simply have no idea as to where and/or how to begin any kind of meaningful discourse with Republican leaders that will provide much-needed outcomes that will help augment the Black community.

Simply put, Black leaders have no skills, no ideas, and strategy to build any kind of meaningful relationship with Republicans. Because of this reality, liberal Black leaders find it easier to preach doom and gloom for Blacks anytime Republicans have political power in the House and Senate as we have witnessed during the recent elections.

Sadly, liberal Black leaders must know that many Republican policies would benefit Black people. However, to admit this truthfulness, these liberal leaders would rather preach the harm of Republican policy in order to keep their inept oath to a few White Democrats.

Anytime a Black leader tells you we are harmed because of the Republican, you ought to tell him to move his butt over and get out of town, because we need a Black leader who has the skills to be nonpartisan, one with the ability to look at Republican policies, get involved in those policies, and help shape our future.

If you can't be nonpartisan, if you are lost, then get out of Dodge and let the Black Republicans be our voice.

The Black Republican can tell you how cutting spending will help Black people. The Black Republican will tell you how shooting down government regulations will help build stronger Black businesses in our community, allowing private Black business to employ Black people.

The Black Republican will move the Black agenda through the House and Senate controlled by Republicans. The Black Republican leader will do all of this and much more. You have to agree that this fight sounds a lot better opposed to the liberal Black leader telling you that we are doomed to all of these policies.

We need a Black leader that is not afraid to tell Democrats how their build-yourself-up-and-we-will-knock-you-down policies are bad news for Blacks. Anything you do, Democrats will knock you down.

You go to college, and you'll pay taxes on books. You get a raise and make more money, and the Democrats place you in a higher tax bracket. You buy a house, and year after year the taxes on the property rise, rise and rise.

The Democrats' best policy is what I call the build-yourself-up-and-we-will-knock-you-down policy. Try to start a business, and we will throw thousands of obstacles in your way, such as this fee, this licenses fee, this regulation.

We need strong Black leadership to tell the Democrats to knock this evilness off. It's not going to come from a liberal Black leader. Liberal Black leaders have it wrong. The Democrat bureaucracy is destroying Black people. This is our fear, not Republicans.

The enemy to Blacks has and continues to be wasteful spending. This wasteful spending sustains the Democrat build-you-up-knock-you-down policy.

Republicans are in control. Republicans have the power. I fully expect Republican officials (like the Democrats) to flex their muscles to full expansion.

Republicans will bring new solutions. Over the next two years, Republicans will move policy to influence votes. Republicans will end wasteful programs. Republicans will call on liberals to justify every wasteful spending.

The Republican Agenda will have a big impact on the lives of Black people over the next few years. Do you want a crybaby leader? No. You want a Black Republican leader, one who can motivate you and encourage you in using Republican policies towards self-reliance.

Lucky Rosenbloom welcomes reader responses to 612-661-0923, email him at l.rosenbloom@yahoo.com, or call his weekly update line for encouragement at 612-387-4546.